KT-443-857

*To Sarah B – a great friend,*
*and a truly super geek*

Thanks to:

Gaby Morgan and Rachel Kellehar at
Macmillan – for edits and encouragment
  Al Murphy – illustrator and arty Murphy
  Lorna, Heath, Julie, Scarlett, Daisy and
Brodie Murphy – arty Murphys, all
  Mum & Dad – as always
  Heather, Sean, Austin and Ka'ge (the cats
were particularly 'helpful' on this one)
  Paul, Jodie and wee Leo Davey –
congratulations! Maybe he'll be a scientist . . .

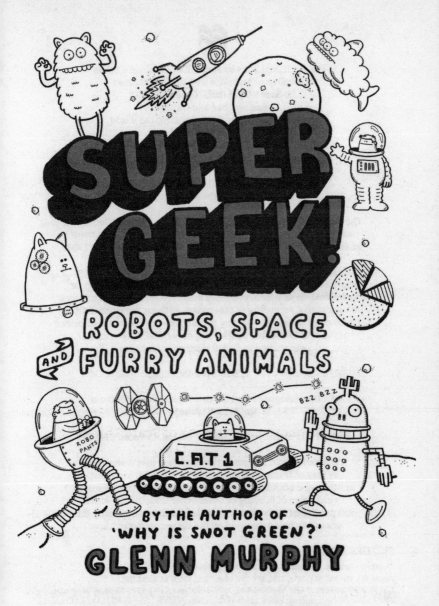

# SUPER GEEK!

## ROBOTS, SPACE and FURRY ANIMALS

BY THE AUTHOR OF
'WHY IS SNOT GREEN?'
## GLENN MURPHY

ILLUSTRATED BY AL MURPHY

MACMILLAN CHILDREN'S BOOKS

First published 2013 by Macmillan Children's Books
a division of Macmillan Publishers Limited
20 New Wharf Road, London N1 9RR
Basingstoke and Oxford
Associated companies throughout the world
www.panmacmillan.com

ISBN 978-1-4472-2732-8

A CIP catalogue record for this book is available from
the British Library.

Printed and bound by CPI Group (UK) Ltd, Croydon CR0 4YY

## PICTURE CREDITS

t = top; b = bottom; r = right, l = left, SS = Shutterstock

Pages: 9tl, 9tr, 9bl, 9br, 12tr, 12bl, 18t, 79t, 79ct, 79cb, 79b & 85 NASA/JPL;
12tl SS/MichaelTaylor; 12br SS/CVADRAT; 19b SS/ApTone; 25tl & 113tl SS/BlueRingMedia;
25tr & 113cr SS/Lightspring; 25bl & 113cb SS/buruhtan; 25br & 113br SS/CLIPAREA I Custom
Media; 28tl & 116 SS/Oleksii Natykach; 28tr & SS/Photobank; 28bl & 28br SS/Sebastian
Kaulitzki; 41tl & 140t SS/Vitaly Korovin; 41tr & 140ct SS/Piti Tan; 41bl & 140cb SS/kzww;
41br & 140b SS/aarows; 44tl & 145ct Geminoid Japan; 44tr & 145b Hiroshi Ishiguro Osaka
University; 44bl & 145t Wikimedia Commons/Laura Cervantes Roura; 44br & 145cb Courtesy
of Geminoid.DK Henrik Sharfe; 50t SS/catwalker; 51b SS/ilterriorm; 57tl & 171t SS/Against star;
57tr & 171ct SS/Andreas Meyer; 57bl & 171cb SS/little_Carol; 57br & 171b SS/cbpix;
60tl SS/Edward Westmacott; 60tr & 176 SS/Mariusz S. Jurgielewicz; 60bl SS/Tony Wear;
60br SS/yxowert;  66t Dr Arthur Anker; 67c Wikimedia Commons/Nyctimene Robinsoni.

# CONTENTS

# Introduction

It is the twenty-first century, and ours is a world ruled by **science** and **technology**.

Gone are the days when we hid our nerdy knowledge of computers.

No more must we cower behind our desks when we talk of androids and space travel.

It's a lightning-fast world, where new animal species are found every week, new technologies invented every minute and new web updates sent every second.

Without us, humanity has no hope of keeping up. The world *needs* us nerds. It cannot survive without the wisdom of the quick-witted geek.

But how much do *YOU* really know about the science that matters?

Could **you** tell a *dik-dik* from a *dugong*?

Do **you** know the difference between an *asteroid* and a *dwarf planet*?

Could **you** tell us what an *android* is, where your *phalanges* are or how many *bones* are in the average human body?

Challenge yourself. Challenge your friends. Only the true boffs will pass the test. Only the wise will succeed.

Only one shall be crowned . . .

SuperGeek!

# How to use this book

*SuperGeek!* is both a book *and* a game.

As a book, you can read it, cover to cover, or you can dip in and out, starting with the chapter or theme you're most interested in. After reading a question, choose an answer, then turn to the Answers section in the second half of the book to check your choice and learn more.

There are more than 160 questions in this book, arranged into four themed chapters, with puzzles and fun stuff in between. Along the way, you'll learn all sorts of fascinating things about:

- astronomy and space exploration
- the human body
- robots, computers and digital technology
- animal families and behaviour.

Before long, you'll be stunning your friends and relatives with your new-found knowledge. Read the whole set of SuperGeek! books, and become a mighty brainbox to be reckoned with!

But you can also play this book like a game – trying to get the highest quiz score possible, and perhaps earn yourself the coveted SuperGeek! title.

So who should you play it with, and how do you play?

As for the *who* – that's entirely up to you.

- You can play with friends, either head-to-head, or in teams.
- You can play with your family, calling out the question from the back seat of the car during a road trip.
- You can play with your classmates, pitting one half of the class against the other.
- You can even play alone – pitting your wits against the clock, rather than an opponent.

*How* you play the game depends on the number of players, and whether you're playing in teams, or individually. To find out more about how to play SuperGeek! – including how to score and rank your players – turn to page 189.

In any case, I hope you enjoy this book. A whole world of geek-tastic knowledge awaits you. So whether you're reading, playing or battling, it's time to turn the page and **get stuck in** . . .

# QUESTIONS

## PART ONE: ASTRONOMY AND SPACE EXPLORATION

Do you know your *comets* from your *asteroids*? Your *red dwarfs* from your *blue giants*? Your *dwarf planets* from your *shepherd moons*?

Do you have real, geek-level Space knowledge?

Let's find out . . .

Answers start on page 69.

# SUPERGEEK: QUESTIONS

## A: MEGA-BRAIN QUESTIONS

**1.  Mars is home to the solar system's largest mountain. What is it called?**

a)  Mount Mars
b)  Mount Olympus
c)  Olympus Mars
d)  Olympus Mons

**2.  Jupiter is famous for its Great Red Spot. But which planet boasts a Great Dark Spot?**

a)  Venus
b)  Saturn
c)  Uranus
d)  Neptune

**3.  How many of the eight planets in our solar system have rings?**

a)  one
b)  two
c)  four
d)  all of them

**4. What makes the planet Uranus so unusual?**

a) it spins backwards
b) it spins on its side
c) it spins faster than all the other planets
d) it's the only one named after a body part

**5. Which planet was once thought to be the Earth's twin?**

a) Mars
b) Venus
c) Jupiter
d) Neptune

**6. Mars has two moons. What are they called?**

a) Phobos and Deimos
b) Romulus and Remus
c) Charon and Nix
d) Marvin and Melinda

**7.** On which planet do temperatures reach over 450°C by day, but plummet to –150°C every night?

a) Mercury
b) Venus
c) Uranus
d) none of them

**8.** Which two planets have more than 60 moons each?

a) Mars and Jupiter
b) Jupiter and Saturn
c) Saturn and Uranus
d) Uranus and Neptune

**9.** Which of the following is NOT a moon found within our solar system?

a) Skoll
b) Pandora
c) Hoth
d) Margaret

**10.** What are Saturn's rings made of?

a) glass
b) metal
c) captured asteroids
d) shattered moons

# B: PICTURE PUZZLE 1

**What is it?**
Name the astronomical objects in each of these pictures:

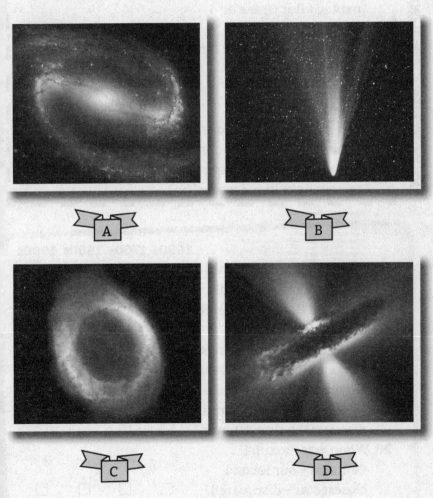

A

B

C

D

# C: QUICK-FIRE QUESTIONS

|  | 1 | 6 | 12 | 24 |
|---|---|---|---|---|
| 11. How many planets are NOT named after Greek or Roman gods? | ☐ | ☐ | ☐ | ☐ |
| 12. How many astronauts have walked on the Moon? | ☐ | ☐ | ☐ | ☐ |
| 13. How many astronauts have flown to the Moon? | ☐ | ☐ | ☐ | ☐ |
| 14. How many planets in our solar system have moons? | ☐ | ☐ | ☐ | ☐ |
| 15. How many planets in our solar system have liquid water? | ☐ | ☐ | ☐ | ☐ |

|  | 1600s | 1700s | 1800s | 1900s |
|---|---|---|---|---|
| 16. During which century was the Uranus discovered? | ☐ | ☐ | ☐ | ☐ |
| 17. When did Galileo Galilei first spot Jupiter's moons? | ☐ | ☐ | ☐ | ☐ |
| 18. When were Saturn's rings first spotted by Christiaan Huygens? | ☐ | ☐ | ☐ | ☐ |
| 19. When did Giovanni Piazzi discover the first asteroid? | ☐ | ☐ | ☐ | ☐ |
| 20. When was Proxima Centauri – our second-closest star – discovered? | ☐ | ☐ | ☐ | ☐ |

|  | 10 | 20 | 200 | 2,000 |
|---|---|---|---|---|
| 21. How many Earth-like planets have been found in our galaxy to date? | ☐ | ☐ | ☐ | ☐ |
| 22. How many days would it take a manned spacecraft to reach Mars? | ☐ | ☐ | ☐ | ☐ |
| 23. How many billion stars are there in the Milky Way? | ☐ | ☐ | ☐ | ☐ |
| 24. How many times further from the Sun is Saturn, compared with the Earth? | ☐ | ☐ | ☐ | ☐ |
| 25. How many times further from the Sun is Uranus, compared with the Earth? | ☐ | ☐ | ☐ | ☐ |

|  | 1969 | 1971 | 1983 | 1997 |
|---|---|---|---|---|
| 26. When did the *Apollo 11* mission land on the Moon? | ☐ | ☐ | ☐ | ☐ |
| 27. In what year did Sally K. Ride become NASA's first female astronaut? | ☐ | ☐ | ☐ | ☐ |
| 28. In what year did astronauts first drive a lunar buggy on the Moon? | ☐ | ☐ | ☐ | ☐ |
| 29. When did the Mars Pathfinder probe land on Mars? | ☐ | ☐ | ☐ | ☐ |
| 30. When was the world's first space station launched? | ☐ | ☐ | ☐ | ☐ |

# D: PICTURE PUZZLE 2

**Odd one out**

Which one doesn't belong here, and why?

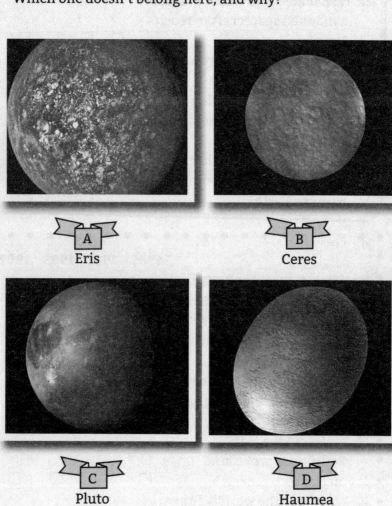

A
Eris

B
Ceres

C
Pluto

D
Haumea

# E: MORE MEGA-BRAIN QUESTIONS

**31. What are *white dwarf*, *blue giant* and *pulsar* all types of?**

a) star
b) planet
c) galaxy
d) spacecraft

**32. What kind of galaxy is the Milky Way?**

a) spiral
b) barred spiral
c) irregular
d) chocolate

**33. What happened to NASA's ill-fated *Apollo 13* mission?**

a) it failed to launch
b) it blew up on the launchpad
c) it launched, but didn't make it to the Moon
d) it made it to the Moon, but failed to land

**34. Neil Armstrong was – famously – the first person to set foot on the Moon. But who was the last?**

a) Buzz Aldrin
b) Michael Collins
c) Gene Cernan
d) Jim Lovell

**35. What does SETI stand for?**

a) Space Engineering and Teaching International
b) Search for Extra-Terrestrial Information
c) Search for Extra-Terrestrial Intelligence
d) Search for Extra-Terrestrial Invertebrates

**36. What is the name for the boundary of a black hole, from which nothing (even light) can escape?**

a) the singularity
b) the event horizon
c) the black boundary
d) the time horizon

**37. What name do astronomers give to an exploding star?**

a) pulsar
b) quasar
c) neutron star
d) supernova

**38. What is the name given to two stars that orbit each other?**

a) binary stars
b) dual stars
c) multiple stars
d) moon stars

**39. Which galaxy – also known as M31 and NGC 224 – is the closest spiral galaxy to our own?**

a) the Sombrero Galaxy
b) the Andromeda Galaxy
c) the Whirlpool Galaxy
d) the Sunflower Galaxy

**40. All known galaxies have an official name that begins with 'NGC'. What does NGC stand for?**

a) National Galaxy Chart
b) New Galactic Catalogue
c) New General Catalogue
d) Numbered Galaxy Coordinate

# ASTRO PUZZLER

Use the clues to complete this tricky astronomical crossword puzzle.

**Across**

2) Spinning neutron star that releases regular radio-wave pulses (6)

5) Target for the *NASA Messenger* mission, launched in August 2004 (7)

6) Moon of Pluto, named after mythical ferryman of the Underworld (6)

8) Surname of second man to set foot on the Moon (6)

9) Planet orbited by moons Europa, Ganymede and Io (7)

**Down**

1) Roving robot probe that landed on Mars in August 2012 (9)

3) Surname of the first man in Space (7)

4) Cloud of interstellar gas, often left behind after a supernova (6)

5) Soviet space station that orbited the Earth from 1986–2001 (3)

7) Egg-shaped dwarf planet with moons Hi'aka and Namaka (6)

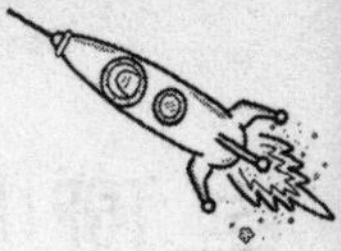

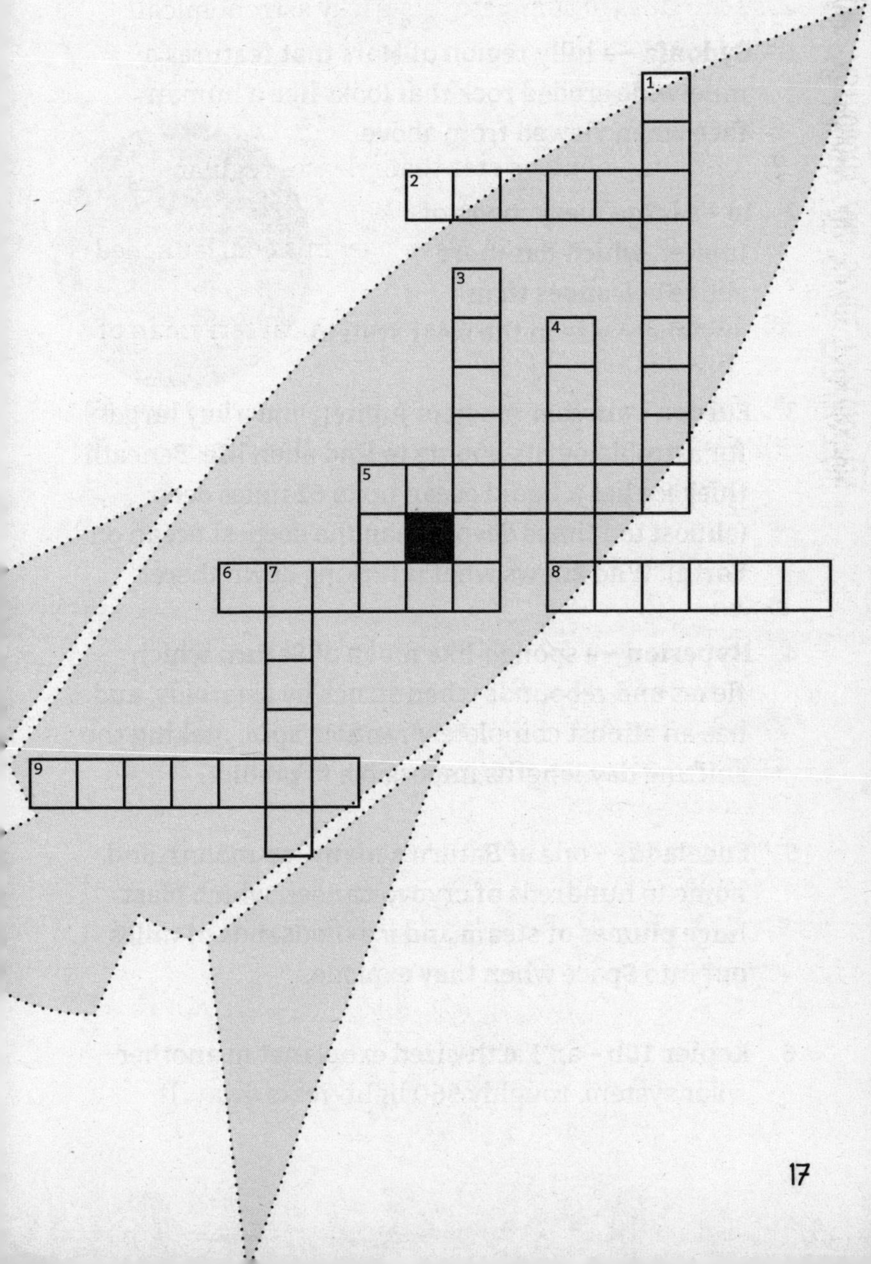
1
2
3
4
5
6
7
8
9

# TOP 10 COOLEST PLACES IN THE UNIVERSE

1. **Cydonia** – a hilly region of Mars that features a mile-wide eroded rock that looks like a human face when viewed from above.

2. **Io** – a large, fiery moon of Jupiter, which has more active volcanoes than anywhere else in the solar system.

3. **Europa** – another moon of Jupiter, and a key target for astrobiologists hoping to find alien life. Beneath thick ice lies a liquid ocean up to 62 miles deep (almost ten times deeper than the deepest ocean on Earth). Who knows what is lurking down there?

4. **Hyperion** – a sponge-like moon of Saturn which flexes and rebounds when struck by asteroids, and has an almost completely random spin, making the shifting day lengths impossible to predict.

5. **Enceladus** – one of Saturn's many ice-moons, and home to hundreds of cryovolcanoes, which blast huge plumes of steam and ice thousands of miles out into Space when they explode.

6. **Kepler 10b** – an Earth-sized exoplanet in another solar system, roughly 560 light-years away. It

orbits roughly twenty times closer to its sun than Mercury does to ours. It gets pretty toasty on its surface. Around 1,600°C to be precise, which is hot enough to melt glass.

7. **TrES-4** – a massive exoplanet, which is almost twice the size of Jupiter. Planets this large should not, in theory, exist at all. This gas giant has such a low density that bits of it drift off into Space as it orbits, giving the planet a long, trailing tail.

8. **HD 188753 Ab (aka Tatooine)** – a Jupiter-sized planet orbiting within a triple-star system. In other words, you could see three suns from its surface – like the planet Tatooine (home to Luke Skywalker) in *Star Wars*.

9. **GJ 1214b (aka Waterworld)** – a so-called 'Super-Earth' (a planet with a mass somewhere between that of Earth and Neptune) in a system just 40 light-years from ours. It has a solid centre and a watery surface. Alien mermaids, anyone?

10. **PSR J1719-1438b (aka the Diamond Planet)** – originally a star itself in a two-star, or binary system, it became a super-dense planet after the other star, known as a pulsar, sucked most of the mass from its body. The carbon-rich core left behind was at such high pressure that it crystallized into a single, giant diamond.

# QUESTIONS

## PART TWO: BLOOD AND GUTS

Could you tell us where your *sternum* is? Which organ fails during a *cardiac arrest*? How long your *femur* is? How many *phalanges* the average person has?

Time to get physical, and test your body knowledge...

Answers start on page 101.

# SUPERGEEK: QUESTIONS

## A: MEGA-BRAIN QUESTIONS

**1. What is your appendix for?**

a) it helps you breathe
b) it helps you digest food
c) it helps you fight off infections
d) nothing – it's useless

**2. What do tendons do in the body?**

a) connect muscles to bones
b) connect muscles to skin
c) connect bones to bones
d) connect muscles to muscles

**3. How many bones are there in an adult human body?**

a) 50–100
b) 100–200
c) 200–250
d) 300–350

4. How many muscles are there in an adult human body?

a) 100–200
b) 200–300
c) 300–600
d) 600–900

5. What are the four major blood types?

a) A, B, C, D
b) A, B, C, O
c) A, B, O, AB
d) A, B, X, Y

6. If you were 120 cm tall, how long would your femur bone be?

a) 15 cm
b) 30 cm
c) 60 cm
d) 90 cm

**7. Which of the following can give you asthma?**

a) dust
b) pollen
c) cat hairs
d) none of the above

**8. Why do old people seem to shrink as they age?**

a) because their legs get shorter with age
b) because their spines bend and shorten with age
c) because their bodies are growing in reverse
d) because they wear flatter shoes

**9. How long could the average person survive without water?**

a) a few hours
b) a few days
c) a few weeks
d) a few months

**10. What type of tooth is a wisdom tooth?**

a) canine
b) incisor
c) premolar
d) molar

# B: PICTURE PUZZLE 1

**What is it?**

Name the organs in each of these pictures:

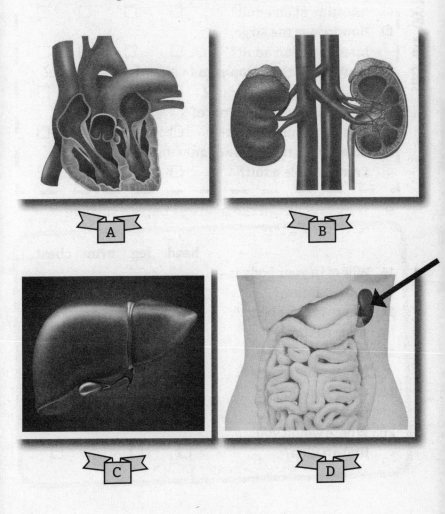

A

B

C

D

# C: QUICK-FIRE QUESTIONS

|  | 30 cm | 50 cm | 1.5 m | 7 m |
|---|---|---|---|---|
| 11. How long is the small intestine of an adult? | ☐ | ☐ | ☐ | ☐ |
| 12. How long is the large intestine of an adult? | ☐ | ☐ | ☐ | ☐ |
| 13. How long is the oesophagus of an average male adult? | ☐ | ☐ | ☐ | ☐ |
| 14. How long is the humerus of an average male adult? | ☐ | ☐ | ☐ | ☐ |
| 15. How long is the femur of an average male adult? | ☐ | ☐ | ☐ | ☐ |

|  | head | leg | arm | chest |
|---|---|---|---|---|
| 16. Where in your body is your cranium? | ☐ | ☐ | ☐ | ☐ |
| 17. Where in your body is your maxilla? | ☐ | ☐ | ☐ | ☐ |
| 18. Where would you find your sternum? | ☐ | ☐ | ☐ | ☐ |
| 19. Where would you find a fibula? | ☐ | ☐ | ☐ | ☐ |
| 20. Where would you find an ulna? | ☐ | ☐ | ☐ | ☐ |

| | heart | lung | kidney | liver |
|---|:---:|:---:|:---:|:---:|
| 21. Which organ is affected by a pulmonary disease? | ☐ | ☐ | ☐ | ☐ |
| 22. Which organ fails during a cardiac arrest? | ☐ | ☐ | ☐ | ☐ |
| 23. Which organ is infected when you have hepatitis? | ☐ | ☐ | ☐ | ☐ |
| 24. Which renal organ filters waste from your bloodstream? | ☐ | ☐ | ☐ | ☐ |
| 25. Which organ has four chambers and is made of muscle? | ☐ | ☐ | ☐ | ☐ |

| | arms | leg | stomach | chest |
|---|:---:|:---:|:---:|:---:|
| 26. Where are your biceps brachii muscles? | ☐ | ☐ | ☐ | ☐ |
| 27. Where are your biceps femoralis muscles? | ☐ | ☐ | ☐ | ☐ |
| 28. Where are your abdominal muscles? | ☐ | ☐ | ☐ | ☐ |
| 29. Where are your pectoral muscles? | ☐ | ☐ | ☐ | ☐ |
| 30. What moves when you contract your quadriceps? | ☐ | ☐ | ☐ | ☐ |

# D: PICTURE PUZZLE 2

## Odd one out

Which one doesn't belong here, and why?

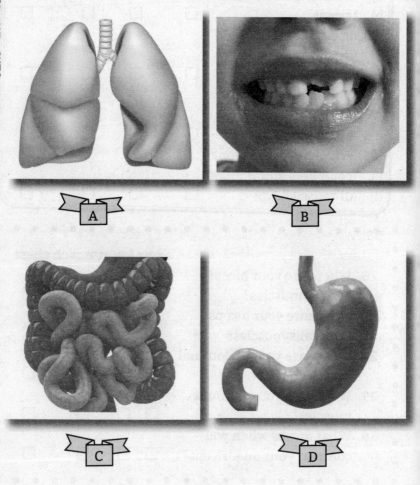

A

B

C

D

# E: MORE MEGA-BRAIN QUESTIONS

**31.  What is the largest muscle in the human body?**

a)  biceps
b)  triceps
c)  deltoid
d)  gluteus maximus

**32.  What job does the liver do within the body?**

a)  it produces and stores energy
b)  it stores essential vitamins and minerals
c)  it removes poisons and toxins from the blood
d)  all of the above

**33.  Which of the following is NOT part of your respiratory system?**

a)  trachea
b)  pancreas
c)  diaphragm
d)  bronchi

**34. Anaemia, thalassaemia and haemophilia are all diseases of the what?**

a) skin
b) brain
c) eye
d) blood

**35. Where in the body would you find your phalanges?**

a) inside the lungs
b) inside the brain
c) in your intestines
d) in your hands and feet

**36. Which type of blood cell fights off bacteria and viruses?**

a) red blood cell
b) white blood cell
c) blue blood cell
d) platelet

**37. Which bone is the odd one out?**

a) scapula
b) humerus
c) coccyx
d) clavicle

**38. What are vaccines made from?**

a) plants
b) fungi
c) lab chemicals
d) viruses and bacteria

**39. What is the more common name for *cerumen*?**

a) bile
b) bogeys
c) ear wax
d) belly-button fluff

**40. Which of the following diseases is NOT caused by a virus?**

a) measles
b) TB (tuberculosis)
c) Ebola
d) influenza

# BODY PUZZLER

Use the clues to complete this tricky anatomical crossword.

**Across**
2) Medical word for kneecap (7)
4) Teeth between the incisors and premolars (7)
5) Common name for the mandible (7)
8) Blood cells responsible for clotting (9)
9) The heart's lower chambers (10)

**Down**
1) Where your humerus, clavicle and scapula meet (8)
3) Muscle opposite your biceps (7)
6) The heart's upper chambers (5)
7) Word following sweat, thyroid and salivary (5)
10) Medical term for the top part of your skull (7)

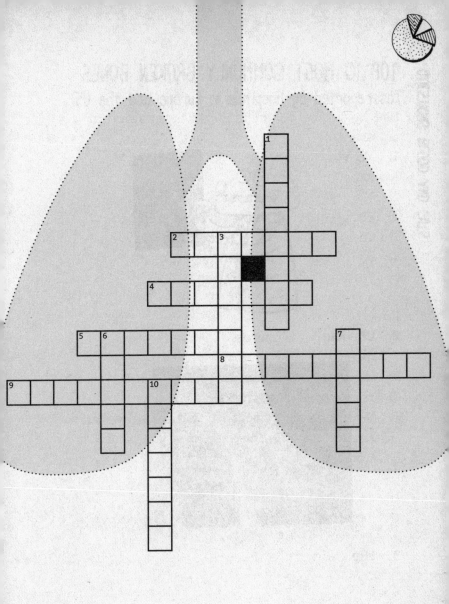

# TOP 10 MOST COMMONLY BROKEN BONES
(as reported by hospitals in Europe and the US)

1. Wrist

2. Clavicle

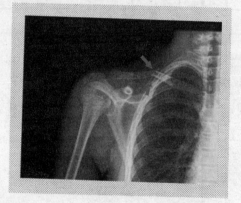

3. Hip

4. Finger

5.  Toe

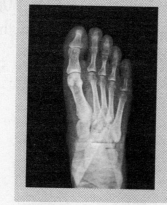

6.  Foot

7.  Ankle

8.  Arm

9.  Nose

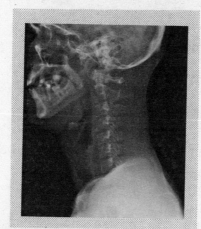

10. Jaw

Have you broken any of these? (No bonus points if you have, I'm afraid!)

# QUESTIONS

## PART THREE: ROBOTS AND DIGITAL TECHNOLOGY

Do you speak *JAVA* or *PYTHON*? Know your *CPU* from your *VDU*? Your *ASIMO* from your *Roomba*?

Know how many bytes are in a megabyte, a gigabyte and a terabyte?

The true test of the tech-savvy SuperGeek starts here . . .

Answers start on page 129.

# SUPERGEEK: QUESTIONS

## A: MEGA-BRAIN QUESTIONS

**1.** Who invented the first computer?

a) Leonardo da Vinci
b) Charles Babbage
c) Bill Gates
d) Steve Jobs

**2.** How many bytes are there in a gigabyte (GB)?

a) 1,000
b) 1,000,000 (1 million)
c) 1,000,000,000 (1 billion)
d) 1,000,000,000,000 (1 trillion)

**3.** As of 2012, which country was home to the world's most powerful supercomputer?

a) China
b) USA
c) Japan
d) Malaysia

4. The *Apollo 11* Guidance Computer landed the first men on the Moon. How much memory did it have?

a) about 2 kilobytes
b) about 2 megabytes
c) about 2 gigabytes
d) about 2 terabytes

5. In computer programmer speak, what is 'debugging'?

a) removing errors from a program
b) removing viruses from a computer
c) removing faulty hardware from a computer
d) removing insects from a computer

6. Which of the following is NOT a real computer programming language?

a) BASIC
b) TRICKY
c) JAVA
d) PYTHON

**7.  Which of these is NOT a type of computer virus?**

a) Worm
b) Mole
c) Bootsector
d) Trojan horse

**8.  What was the name of the computer that beat chess champion Garry Kasparov in 1997?**

a) Chess Champ
b) Deep Thought
c) Deep Moves
d) Deep Blue

**9.  What is the name of the standard test for Artificial Intelligence (AI)?**

a) the IQ Test
b) the Turing Test
c) the Asimov Test
d) the Einstein Test

**10. Which country's population has the highest percentage of Internet users?**

a) Japan
b) China
c) USA
d) Iceland

# B: PICTURE PUZZLE 1

**What is it?**

All these computer components have abbreviated
three-letter names (e.g. ABC, XYZ). Name each of them:

A

B

C

D

41

# C: QUICK-FIRE QUESTIONS

|  | 1951 | 1971 | 1977 | 1978 |
|---|---|---|---|---|
| 11. When was the first mobile-phone network activated? | ☐ | ☐ | ☐ | ☐ |
| 12. When was the first colour TV programme broadcast? | ☐ | ☐ | ☐ | ☐ |
| 13. When was the first email sent? | ☐ | ☐ | ☐ | ☐ |
| 14. When was the first microchip built? | ☐ | ☐ | ☐ | ☐ |
| 15. When did the first global Internet first come online? | ☐ | ☐ | ☐ | ☐ |

|  | Japan | USA | UK | Other |
|---|---|---|---|---|
| 16. Which country invented the video game? | ☐ | ☐ | ☐ | ☐ |
| 17. Which country built the first android? | ☐ | ☐ | ☐ | ☐ |
| 18. Where did the inventors of the TV and phone come from? | ☐ | ☐ | ☐ | ☐ |
| 19. Which country invented CDs and DVDs? | ☐ | ☐ | ☐ | ☐ |
| 20. Where was the USB flash drive invented? | ☐ | ☐ | ☐ | ☐ |

| | 1983 | 1988 | 1991 | 2001 |
|---|---|---|---|---|
| 21. In what year was the very first iPod sold? | ☐ | ☐ | ☐ | ☐ |
| 22. When was the first web browser created? | ☐ | ☐ | ☐ | ☐ |
| 23. When did the first digital camera go on sale? | ☐ | ☐ | ☐ | ☐ |
| 24. When did CDs begin to outsell records and cassettes? | ☐ | ☐ | ☐ | ☐ |
| 25. When did the first laptop computer go on sale? | ☐ | ☐ | ☐ | ☐ |

| | Europe | N. America | Asia | Africa |
|---|---|---|---|---|
| 26. Which continent has the most Internet users? | ☐ | ☐ | ☐ | ☐ |
| 27. Which continent is home to one-fifth of Internet users? | ☐ | ☐ | ☐ | ☐ |
| 28. Which continent is home to 12 per cent of Internet users? | ☐ | ☐ | ☐ | ☐ |
| 29. Which continent is home to just 6 per cent of Internet users? | ☐ | ☐ | ☐ | ☐ |
| 30. On which continent do 80 per cent of people have Internet access? | ☐ | ☐ | ☐ | ☐ |

# D: PICTURE PUZZLE 2

**Odd one out**

Which one doesn't belong here, and why?

A

B

C

D

# E: MORE MEGA-BRAIN QUESTIONS

**31. What are female androids called?**

a) fembots
b) femoids
c) gynoids
d) girloids

**32. How many robots are working in the world today?**

a) about 9,000
b) about 90,000
c) about 900,000
d) About 9,000,000

**33. The word 'robot' comes from the Czech word
  *robota*. What does it mean?**

a) hard work
b) fake man
c) metal man
d) clever machine

**34. What are the four basic parts of a robot?**

a) body, brain, arms, legs
b) body, brain, controllers, motors
c) body, controller, sensors, actuators
d) body, controller, sensors, circuits

**35. ASIMO is one of the world's most advanced robots. Which Japanese engineering company built him?**

a) Sony
b) Honda
c) Hitachi
d) Toyota

**36. Which of the following is NOT a pet robot?**

a) AIBO
b) PARO
c) PLEO
d) BIG DOG

**37. Which of the following aquatic animals have real, robotic counterparts?**

a) shark
b) lobster
c) octopus
d) all of the above

**38. What is the most common use for industrial (factory) robots worldwide?**

a) carrying stuff
b) assembling
c) welding
d) cutting

**39. What is the most common use for military robots worldwide?**

a) carrying stuff
b) bomb disposal
c) spying
d) fighting

**40. What's special about British robotics professor Kevin Warwick?**

a) he built the first British robot
b) he built a robot version of himself
c) he's the world's first robot teacher
d) he's the world's first cyborg

# TECHNO PUZZLER

Use the clues to complete this tricky, technology-themed crossword.

**Across**

4) Frighteningly realistic 'twin' android, built to look like its owner (8)
5) Unit of memory equal to 1,000,000 bytes (8)
8) Living person or animal with robotic enhancements (6)
9) What the 'h' in 'http' stands for (9)

**Down**

1) Firefox and Google Chrome are both types of this (7)
2) What the 'P' in 'CPU' stands for (10)
3) Software company that created Windows, Word and Internet Explorer (9)
6) Makers of the MacBook, iPod and iPhone (5)
7) Flat, touch-sensitive alternative to the computer mouse (8)

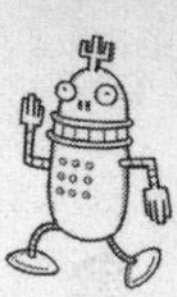

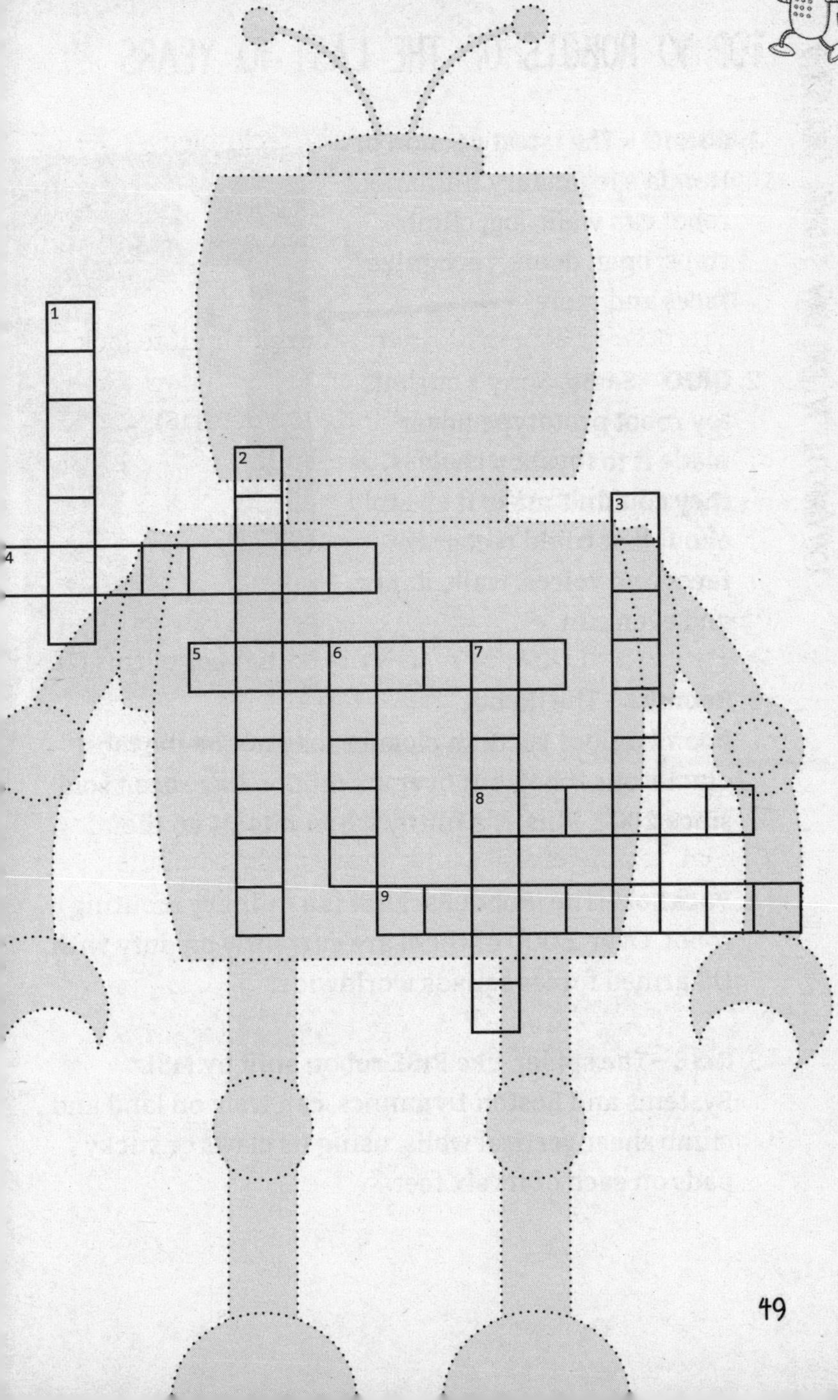
1
2
3
4
5
6
7
8
9

# TOP 10 ROBOTS OF THE LAST 10 YEARS

1. **ASIMO** – The latest version of Honda's legendary humanoid robot can walk, jog, climb steps, open doors, recognize faces and more.

2. **QRIO** – Sadly, Sony's curious toy robot prototype never made it to toyshop shelves, as they couldn't make it cheaply enough. It could recognize faces and voices, walk, dance, and even run.

3. **Roomba** – The iRobot Roomba floor vacuum cleaner may not be the most glamorous robot, but over six million have been sold since 2002. Plus, it's funny when cats sit on them.

4. **PackBot** – The iRobot PackBot is a military scouting robot. Over 2,000 of them are currently on duty with US armed forces squads worldwide.

5. **RiSE** – The spider-like RiSE robot, built by MSL Systems and Boston Dynamics, can walk on land and climb sheer vertical walls, using its claws or sticky pads on each of its six feet.

6. **BIG DOG** – The Boston Dynamics BIG DOG is a mechanized, military pack animal. Its shock-absorbing legs keep it balanced on rough terrain and steep slopes.

7. **Rhex** – Also built by Boston Dynamics, Rhex is an amphibious, all-terrain scout robot modelled on a scuttling cockroach. Its six legs allow it to paddle through grass, snow, swamps and open water.

8. **ACM-R5** – This amphibious snakebot, built by the Tokyo Institute of Technology, is a search-and-rescue robot. It's designed to slither and swim into spaces humans and rescue dogs cannot reach.

9. **PLEO** – Ugobe Labs' baby dinosaur is perhaps the most advanced and intelligent toy robot to date. Pleo is is 'born' unable to walk or see, and only later opens his eyes, reacts to sights and sounds, starts to totter around and learns about the world around him. Two Pleos can recognize each other and – depending on whether they're male or female – can argue, fight or fall in love. Ahhhhh.

10. **AIBO** – Sony's lovable robo-dog went offline in 2006, but thousands of them still totter around homes around the globe. There's even an AIBO soccer tournament, for hardcore AIBO fans.

SUPERGEEK QUESTIONS

# QUESTIONS

## PART FOUR: ANIMALS AND ANIMAL BEHAVIOUR

How many legs on a lobster? Where would you find a dik-dik, or an aye-aye, and what would they look like? Which family of animals contains bears, badgers and walruses?

This one's all about animals. But it's no easy ride...

Answers start on page 159.

# SUPERGEEK: QUESTIONS

## A: MEGA-BRAIN QUESTIONS

**1. Which of the following is not a real animal?**

a) sea urchin
b) sea lettuce
c) sea cucumber
d) sea squirt

**2. Box, lion's mane and man-o'-war are all types of what?**

a) spider
b) jellyfish
c) monkey
d) tropical bird

**3. What percentage of all known animal species are insects?**

a) 10 per cent
b) 30 per cent
c) 60 per cent
d) 90 per cent

4. **Which of the following is NOT actually a bug?**

a) pond skater
b) ladybird
c) assassin bug
d) stink bug

5. **Nematodes are the most numerous animals on Earth. What are they?**

a) worms
b) beetles
c) birds
d) bats

6. **Which family of animals are whales most closely related to?**

a) sharks
b) rays
c) hippos
d) crocodiles

7. **What name do zoologists give to the order of animals that includes giant pandas, sea otters, walruses and badgers?**

a) Ursidae
b) Canidae
c) Carnivora
d) Cetacea

**8.   What's the main difference between a manatee and a dugong?**

a)   one is an insect, the other is a mammal
b)   one is a seal, the other is a fish
c)   one's a herbivore, the other is a carnivore
d)   their tails are different shapes

**9.   What are barn, burrowing, spectacled and snowy all types of?**

a)   eel
b)   owl
c)   bat
d)   bear

**10. What do lobsters, earthworms and tarantulas all have in common?**

a)   they're all aquatic animals
b)   they're all arachnids
c)   they're all vertebrates
d)   they're all invertebrates

# B: PICTURE PUZZLE 1

**What is it?**

Name the animals in each of these pictures:

A

B

C

D

# C: QUICK-FIRE QUESTIONS

|  | fish | insect | mammal | bird |
|---|---|---|---|---|
| 11. What kind of animal is an aye-aye? | ☐ | ☐ | ☐ | ☐ |
| 12. what kind of animal is a shrike? | ☐ | ☐ | ☐ | ☐ |
| 13. What kind of animal is a dik-dik? | ☐ | ☐ | ☐ | ☐ |
| 14. What kind of animal is a grouper? | ☐ | ☐ | ☐ | ☐ |
| 15. What kind of animal is a mantid? | ☐ | ☐ | ☐ | ☐ |

|  | 6 | 8 | 10 | 14 |
|---|---|---|---|---|
| 16. How many legs does a **scorpion** have? | ☐ | ☐ | ☐ | ☐ |
| 17. How many legs does a **spider crab** have? | ☐ | ☐ | ☐ | ☐ |
| 18. How many legs would you find on a **wood louse**? | ☐ | ☐ | ☐ | ☐ |
| 19. How many legs does a **flea** have? | ☐ | ☐ | ☐ | ☐ |
| 20. How many legs on a **dung beetle**? | ☐ | ☐ | ☐ | ☐ |

|  | Asia | Australia | Africa | Arctic |
|---|---|---|---|---|
| 21. Where do spiny echidnas live? | ☐ | ☐ | ☐ | ☐ |
| 22. Where do wolverines live? | ☐ | ☐ | ☐ | ☐ |
| 23. Where do mandrills live? | ☐ | ☐ | ☐ | ☐ |
| 24. Where would you find a green water dragon? | ☐ | ☐ | ☐ | ☐ |
| 25. Where would you find a boomslang? | ☐ | ☐ | ☐ | ☐ |

|  | rodent | reptile | cat | ape |
|---|---|---|---|---|
| 26. What kind of animal is a siamang? | ☐ | ☐ | ☐ | ☐ |
| 27. What kind of animal is a coypu? | ☐ | ☐ | ☐ | ☐ |
| 28. What kind of animal is a capybara? | ☐ | ☐ | ☐ | ☐ |
| 29. What kind of animal is a tuatara? | ☐ | ☐ | ☐ | ☐ |
| 30. What kind of animal is a jaguarundi? | ☐ | ☐ | ☐ | ☐ |

# D: PICTURE PUZZLE 2

**Odd one out**

Which one doesn't belong here, and why?

A
lobster

B
horseshoe crab

C
giant spider crab

D
barnacle

# E: MORE MEGA-BRAIN QUESTIONS

**31. How does an archerfish catch its prey?**

a) shoots water at it
b) digs a trap in the riverbed
c) snares it in pond weeds
d) baits it with a worm-like lure on its head

**32. Which is the only type of animal that could survive being dropped in a blender?**

a) sponge
b) starfish
c) jellyfish
d) octopus

**33. Which of the following mammals is venomous?**

a) European mole
b) Eurasian water shrew
c) duck-billed platypus
d) all of the above

**34. How would a Brazilian tapir escape from a jaguar?**

a) outrun it
b) climb a tree
c) dig a hole
d) go snorkelling

**35. How do boas and pythons kill their prey?**

a) by drowning
b) by suffocation
c) by crushing its heart
d) by injecting deadly venom

**36. Which of the following animals does NOT hunt in packs?**

a) lion
b) tiger
c) hyena
d) chimpanzee

**37. What do marsupials have that other types of mammal do not?**

a) hair
b) nipples
c) pouches
d) tails

**38. What are the four most common types of tiger?**

a) Indian, Malayan, Russian and Australian
b) Bengal, Sumatran, Siberian and Tasmanian
c) Indian, Siberian, Malayan and Sumatran
d) Bengal, Siberian, Malayan and Indochinese

**39. Which of the following is NOT a flightless bird?**

a) penguin
b) peacock
c) kiwi
d) kakapo

**40. Which snake has the most deadly venom?**

a) rattlesnake
b) fierce snake
c) king cobra
d) black mamba

# ANIMAL PUZZLER

Use the clues to complete this tricky, zoological crossword.

**Across**

5) Shorter-necked relative of the giraffe (5)
6) Blue, right and humpback are all types of these (5)
7) Furry, flying mammal of the class *Chiroptera* (3)
8) Kangaroos, wallabies and opossums are all members of this pouch-bearing mammal family (10)

**Down**

1) Name given to animals with backbones (11)
2) Wild dog native to Australia (5)
3) Animal class that includes iguanas, basilisks and Komodo dragons (8)
4) Noisy, tree-dwelling bug of the tropics (6)
6) Slimy animal that goes with hook-, round- and earth- (4)
7) Family of animals, also known as Ursidae, which includes black, brown and polar varieties (5)

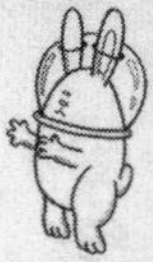

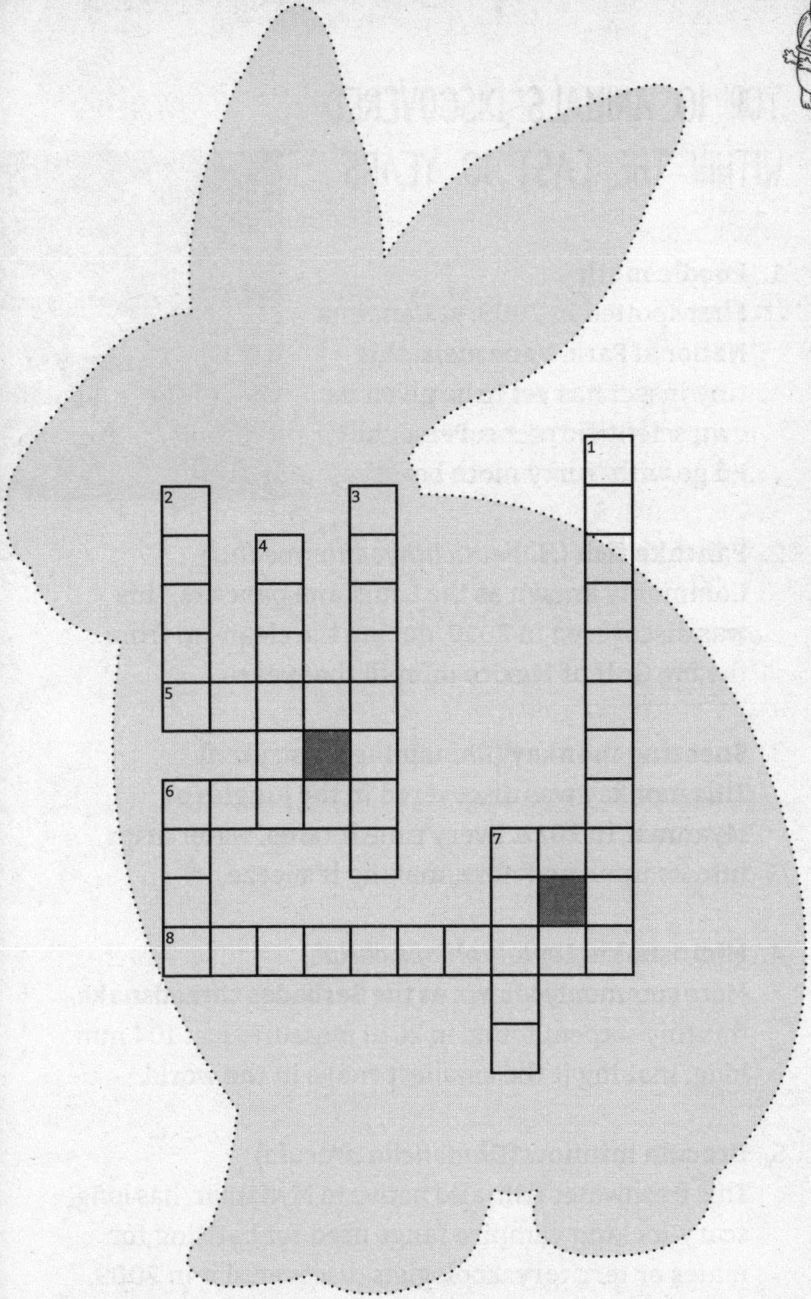
1
2
3
4
5
6
7
8

# TOP 10 ANIMALS DISCOVERED WITHIN THE LAST 10 YEARS

1. **Poodle moth**
   First spotted in 2009, at Canaima National Park, Venezuela, this tiny insect has yet to be given its own scientific name. Personally, I'd go with 'furry moth beast'.

2. **Pancake fish** (*Halieutichthys intermedius*)
   Commonly known as the Louisiana pancake, this was discovered in 2010, during the clean-up from the big Gulf of Mexico oil spill that year.

3. **Sneezing monkey** (*Rhinopithecus strykeri*)
   This monkey was discovered in the jungles of Myanmar in 2012. Every time it rains, water drips into its upturned nose, making it sneeze.

4. **Microsnake** (*Leptotyphlops carlae*)
   More commonly known as the **Barbados threadsnake**, this tiny serpent found in 2010 measures just 104 mm long, making it the smallest snake in the world.

5. **Dracula minnow** (*Danionella dracula*)
   This freshwater fish, also native to Mynamar, has long, scary-looking vampire fangs used for battling for mates or territory. Zoologists discovered it in 2009.

6. **Blue tarantula** (*Pterinopelma sazimai*)
Discovered in the Brazilian rainforest in 2012, this
iridescent blue tarantula seems to glow against the
backdrop of greens in its environment.

7. **Wandering leg sausage** (*Crurifarcimen vagans*)
This fat millipede grows up to 40 cm long, and
was found in 2012 in the mountains of Tanzania.
Its Latin name comes from the words *crus* (leg),
*farcimen* (sausage), and *vagans* (wanderer).

8. **Tube-nosed bat** (*Nyctimene*)
This fruit bat was one of over 200
species discovered during a single
expedition to Papua New Guinea in
2009. It belongs to an entire family
of tube-nosed fruit bats, which
also includes the scary-sounding
'demonic tube-nosed fruit bat'.

9. **Pygmy seahorse** (*Hippocampus satomiae*)
Discovered in 2008 in the coral reefs of Indonesia,
males reach a maximum size of 14 mm, which may
explain why no one had ever spotted one until now.

10. **Mega stick** (*Phobaeticus chani*)
This enormous stick insect was discovered in Borneo
in 2008. At over half a metre long, it's about the
same length as a human arm. It is (by some margin)
the longest.

# ANSWERS

# PART ONE:
# ASTRONOMY AND
# SPACE EXPLORATION

# SUPERGEEK: ANSWERS

>>>>>>>>>>>>>>>>>>>>>>>>>>>>>>>>>>>>>>

## A: MEGA-BRAIN ANSWERS

### 1. (d) Olympus Mons

Mars is home to some of the solar system's most spectacular mountain ranges – many of which dwarf Earth's Himalayas, Rockies and Alps. Its largest mountain, Olympus Mons, is actually an enormous volcano, over **24 km (78,000 feet)** high, that's over **2.5 times** taller than Everest.

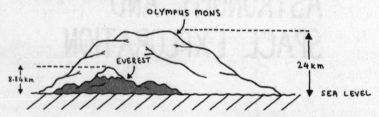

Who knows – maybe one day Mars will become the top holiday destination for mountain climbers worldwide. You've done Everest – now try Olympus Mons!

Actually, provided that you made it safely to Mars – and had a spacesuit and oxygen supply – *climbing* Olympus Mons wouldn't be that hard. That's because the vast, sprawling cone of the volcano is almost thirty times as wide as it is tall. So unlike the steep, jutting slopes of Everest, the sides of Olympus Mons slope upward at a gentle **5 or 6 degrees**.

>>>>>>>>>>>>>>>>>>>>>>>>>>>>>>>>>>>>>>

## 2. (d) Neptune

With Pluto now demoted to *dwarf planet* status, Neptune is our solar system's most distant planet. It lies over **4.5 billion km** – or **30.1 Astronomical Units** – from the Sun. That's so far off it's pretty hard to imagine. But consider this – an **Astronomical Unit (AU)** is equal to about **150 million km**, or the average distance from the Earth to the Sun. So at **30.1 AU**, Neptune lies over **thirty times further** from the Sun than the Earth.

The Great Dark Spot is thought to be a massive rotating storm system that lies high in the planet's atmosphere. But while Jupiter's red spot has been near-stationary on its surface for hundreds of years, Neptune's spot whips around the planet at over 700 miles per hour, and disappears entirely for years at a time.

Being so far away from the Sun, astronomers had assumed that Neptune was a cold, dead world. Instead, they found raging storms and a turbulent atmosphere. In many ways, Neptune made us rethink what was possible in the cold, outer reaches of the solar system.

## 3. (c) four

**Saturn**'s bright, shiny rings are twice as wide as the planet itself, and are clearly visible from Earth with any half-decent telescope. And the rings of **Uranus** were first spotted by powerful Earth-based telescopes in 1977. But before the *Voyager* probes, no one expected to find rings round **Jupiter** or **Neptune**.

It was actually *Voyager 1* that got the first glimpse of Jupiter's ring systems, which are so thin that they are invisible to Earth-based telescopes. In 1979, having flown past the planet, *Voyager 1* turned round and took one final snap of Jupiter. As it did so, a single faint ring was silhouetted against the Sun far behind.

*Voyager 2* was tasked with photographing the ring in more detail when it arrived at Jupiter a few months later. *Voyager 2* found a total of **three** faint rings round Jupiter, and went on to spot **five** more faint rings round Neptune in 1989. Some of Neptune's rings are so faint that sections of them disappear entirely, leaving broken, ghostly **ring arcs** rather than complete rings round the planet.

So thanks to the Voyager probes, now we know: all four **gas giant** planets of the outer solar system – Jupiter, Saturn, Uranus and Neptune – have rings.

## 4. (b) it spins on its side

Uranus is, without doubt, the strangest planet in the solar system. All the planets orbit the Sun in the same direction (anti-clockwise), and all except Venus spin the same way on their vertical axis (also anti-

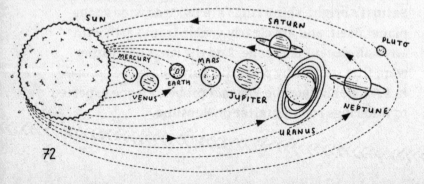

clockwise). But here's the thing – the axis on which Uranus spins isn't vertical. It's more or less horizontal. In effect, then, Uranus **spins on its side**.

The axis of Uranus is tilted at nearly 98 degrees, as if it fell over, or decided to roll, rather than spin through its orbit. When it begins its 84-year orbit, its north pole points directly at the Sun. By the time it's halfway round the Sun, 42 years later, its north pole points directly away from the Sun. As you might imagine, this plays havoc with sunshine and seasons on Uranus. At the poles, you'd get 42 years of daylight and summer, followed by 42 years of darkness and winter. At the equator, a day might last anywhere from 8 hours to 20 years.

So how did Uranus get like that? Our best guess is that it was hit by another planet-sized object, way back in the early formation of the solar system.

## 5. (b) Venus

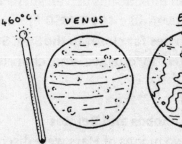

For many years, astronomers have thought of Venus as a 'twin sister' to planet Earth. We now know that the two planets are very, very different, but at first glance this 'twin planet' idea isn't as daft as it seems.

Although it lies much closer to the Sun (at about 0.72 AU, or two-thirds the distance from the Sun to the

Earth), Venus is almost *exactly* the same size as Earth. Venus measures around 12,100 km across, while the Earth is a little wider, at 12,700 km. While the Earth is a little denser and heavier, surface gravity is more or less the same on each planet. And both planets have semi-solid cores, a rocky crust, a solid surface, and a gassy atmosphere. But there the similarities pretty much end.

The atmosphere of Venus is *very* different to that of Earth. Ours is mostly (harmless) nitrogen and (breathable) oxygen, plus less than 1 per cent of toxic, heat-trapping carbon dioxide. The atmosphere of Venus, however, is roughly 96 per cent carbon dioxide and 3 per cent nitrogen, with no free oxygen at all. Not only is this high-pressure atmosphere not *breathable* for humans and other terrestrial animals, it's so thick and heavy that it would *crush* us, long before it choked us.

To make matters worse, all that heat-trapping carbon dioxide has driven surface temperatures up to an oven-like **460°C (850°F)** – hotter than Mercury, which lies far closer to the Sun. So you can add 'roasted' to 'crushed' and 'choked'.

## 6. (a) Phobos and Deimos

The two moons of Mars were discovered by American mathematics professor and astronomer **Asaph Hall** in August 1877. Studying Mars, he spotted two bright 'stars' close to the edge of the planet, which seemed to move *with* the planet, night after night. He soon realized that he had discovered two **moons**, rather than stars.

The moons were later named Phobos and Deimos, after the mythical sons of Mars (known to the ancient Greeks as Ares). In Greek mythology, Phobos (fear) and Deimos (dread) followed Ares into battle, striking terror into the hearts of all soldiers.

The moons of Mars are pretty tiny things. Phobos is only **20 km** wide, and Deimos just **12 km**, making them little bigger than most good-sized towns on Earth. They're small, irregular objects, more like lumpy potatoes than huge, shining orbs.

## 7. (a) Mercury

At an average distance of just **58 million km (0.38 AU)**, Mercury lies far closer to the Sun than the Earth and receives around *nine times* more solar radiation than our planet.

Being so close to the sun, it gets pretty toasty on Mercury during daylight hours. Probes like *Mariner 10* – sent to Mercury as far back as 1974 – have revealed that surface temperatures can reach as high as **450°C** at high noon. However, at night, the surface of Mercury drops to a frosty **–150°C**. But why the huge temperature change?

The answer is that Mercury has no real **atmosphere**. Being so small (Mercury measures just **4,880 km** across – little larger than the Earth's Moon), Mercury's gravitational field isn't strong enough to hold a thick, gassy atmosphere like that of the Earth or Venus. These atmospheres trap heat and leave Venus and the Earth much warmer than they would otherwise be. But on Mercury most of the heat absorbed during the day is lost again at night – as soon as that part of the surface rotates away from the Sun. Without a gassy atmosphere to hold it, the heat just radiates back out into Space.

## 8. (b) Jupiter and Saturn

Sometimes, planets capture passing asteroids with their gravity, turning them into orbiting moons. Some moons were formed from lumps of rocky or icy debris that clumped together around the same time as the planet formed; others from debris smashed out of the planet's surface by a massive impact (this is probably how our own Moon was formed, over five billion years ago).

In any case, the *bigger* the planet, the *stronger* its gravitational field, and the *more moons* it is likely to capture and hold. It makes sense, then, that the two largest planets in the solar system – Jupiter and Saturn – should have collected more moons than all the others.

Mars has just *two* moons. And the Earth, of course, has just the *one* (albeit a very large one). But the **gas giant** planets of the outer solar system, being far more massive, have quite a few more than that:

- **Neptune** has at least **13** moons.
- **Uranus**, being larger, has **27** known moons.
- At the last count, **Saturn** had **62** moons.

- **Jupiter,** by far the largest planet in the solar system, has no less **66** moons.

Some astrobiologists believe there could be **life** on some of these moons. Who knows, maybe we'll find aliens squirming about on Europa before the end of the century . . .

## 9. (c) Hoth

Believe it or not, **Skoll**, **Pandora** and **Margaret** are all proper names for **real** moons – all discovered in our solar system within the last 50 years.

Hoth, on the other hand, is the fictional ice moon occupied by the Rebel Alliance in *Star Wars Episode V: The Empire Strikes Back.* You know: the one where Luke gets knocked off his Tauntaun and mauled by the Hoth Wampa monster.

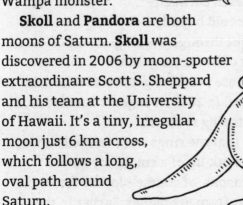

WHAT DO YOU MEAN THIS ISN'T A REAL MOON?

Skoll and Pandora are both moons of Saturn. **Skoll** was discovered in 2006 by moon-spotter extraordinaire Scott S. Sheppard and his team at the University of Hawaii. It's a tiny, irregular moon just 6 km across, which follows a long, oval path around Saturn.

**Pandora** was first spotted by the *Voyager 1* probe when it arrived at Saturn in 1980. An oval object around 140,000 km wide, Pandora is one of Saturn's many **shepherd moons**, which orbit in and around its ring systems, helping the rings hold their position and shape.

**Margaret** – a small, 10 km-wide moon of **Uranus** – was discovered in 2003. It was named after a character from a Shakespeare play: Margaret is a maidservant in *Much Ado About Nothing*.

## 10. (d) shattered moons

Viewed from afar, Saturn's rings look like wide, solid, flat rings round the planet . . .

In fact, the rings of Saturn are made of billions of individual particles – ranging from car-sized boulders of dirty ice to tiny grains of dust and ice

. . . with huge spaces in between them. In fact, you could happily fly a spacecraft straight through the rings at almost any point, with no fear of hitting anything.

So how did all those particles get there? When the *Cassini* probe arrived in 2004, it began a detailed study of the planet and its ring systems.

We now believe that the rings were formed almost entirely from the break-up of a single, icy moon. Saturn has many moons, of course – locked into orbit at various distances from the planet. Earlier in the planet's history, it probably had many more. But one by one, Saturn's powerful gravitational field pulled most of the larger ones inwards, breaking them apart, and drawing them into ring-shaped trails. Later, these trails either clumped back into moons, or drifted into the planet itself.

However, the *last* of these 'doomed moons', it seems, was mostly made of ice. And when it shattered and broke apart, the icy particles left behind formed stable rings round Saturn, sculpted and held in place by the pull of the planet and its various moons.

# B: PICTURE PUZZLE 1

A – **Galaxy.** This one is a barred spiral galaxy.

B – **Comet.** This one is *Comet West*, spotted and named by astronomer Richard West in 1975.

C – **Nebula.** A shell of expanding gases left behind after an explosive supernova.

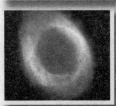

D – **Black Hole.** Black holes themselves are *in*visible, but many shoot out jets of ionized gas, which *are* visible.

# C: QUICK-FIRE ANSWERS

11. **1 planet** Of all eight planets in our solar system, only **Earth** is not named after a Greek or Roman god.

    - **Mercury** was named after the Roman god of travel and trade.
    - **Venus** was named after the Roman goddess of love and beauty.
    - **Mars** was the Roman god of war and (bizarrely) farming.
    - **Jupiter** was the Roman name for *Zeus* – the ancient Greek king of the gods.
    - **Saturn** was the Roman name for *Cronus* – father of Zeus, and god of time.
    - **Uranus**, in turn, was the father of *Cronus* in ancient Greek mythology.
    - **Neptune** was the Roman god of the sea.
    - Finally, **Pluto** (no longer a planet, but it was for a bit) was named after the Roman god of the underworld.

    The name **Earth** comes from the ancient Indo-European word for 'ground'. Seems a bit dull by comparison, doesn't it?

12. **12 astronauts**. In total, 12 NASA astronauts walked on the Moon. They all did it in the same three-and-a-half year stretch, during the *Apollo* missions.

13. **24 astronauts**. Far more people have flown to the Moon than have walked on it. Before *Apollo 11* made the first manned Moon *landing*, the

three-man crews of *Apollo 8* and *Apollo 10* flew to the Moon and *orbited* it without landing. *Apollo 13* didn't land, either, due to an explosion that crippled the landing module on the way there. Each of the *Apollo* missions from *11* to *17* also carried a three-person crew. Three astronauts actually made the trip twice but none of them landed on the Moon more than once.

14. **6 planets**. Of the eight officially recognized planets in our solar system, all but two (Mercury and Venus) have moons.

15. **1 planet**. Frozen water is present on **Mars** and perhaps a few of **Mercury**'s deepest craters, but among the planets only **Earth** has flowing, liquid water. It's possible that some of Jupiter and Saturn's moons – such as **Europa**, **Titan** and **Enceladus** – have liquid water beneath their frozen surfaces, but until we send a probe crashing through to find out we'll never know.

16. **1700s**. The planet **Uranus** was discovered in **1781**, by astronomer William Herschel. (For a while, it was simply called 'Herschel'.)

17. **1600s**. Galileo looked up at Jupiter in **1610**, and spotted its four largest moons lurking on either side. Nowadays, we know these as **Ganymede**, **Callisto**, **Io** and **Europa**. But as a group they're still known as the **Galilean** moons.

18. **1600s**. Dutch mathematician and astronomer **Christiaan Huygens** was the first to describe Saturn's rings after observing them in **1656**.

19. **1800s**. Piazzi spotted the first official asteroid in **1801**. It was **Ceres** – the largest object in the asteroid belt between Mars and Jupiter, and one which has since been reclassified as a **dwarf planet**.

20. **1900s**. **Proxima Centauri** is the closest star to our own planet other than our own (the Sun). It lies just 4.2 light-years (15,000 AU, or 24 trillion miles) away, in the constellation of Centaurus.

21. **2,000 planets**. To date, astronomers have identified at least **2,000** Earth-like planets in our galaxy alone – far more than was previously thought were out there. Since March 2009, we've been scouring the skies using the planet-hunting **Kepler Space Telescope**, training it upon more than 150,000 stars, and looking for the tell-tale 'winks' that indicate a planet moving in front of its host star. This discovery *hugely* increases the odds of finding life elsewhere in our galaxy.

22. **200 days**. How long it takes depends on when you set off, and where Earth and Mars are in their orbits. When Earth and Mars are on the same side of the Sun (a state called *conjunction*), they're a little under 35 million miles apart. When they're on opposite sides of the Sun (a state called *apposition*), it's more like 250 million miles.

23. **200 billion stars**. According to our best estimates, our galaxy, the Milky Way, contains at least 100 billion stars, and perhaps as many as 400 billion stars. **200 billion** seems like a fairly safe bet.

24. **10 times**. The planet **Saturn** lies at a distance of **9.54 AU** from the Sun, meaning that it's almost **10 times** further away from the Sun than the Earth (at **1 AU**). Jupiter lies about halfway between the Sun and Saturn, at about **5 AU.** So Jupiter is roughly five times further from the Sun than the Earth.

25. **20 times**. At an average distance of **19.19 AU**, the planet **Uranus** lies almost *twice* as far from the Sun as Saturn, and **20 times** as far from the Sun as planet Earth. **Neptune**, the most distant planet, lies another **11 AU** beyond Uranus, 30 times further from the Sun than the Earth. The solar system is a pretty roomy place.

26. **1969**. The *Apollo 11* mission was launched on 16 July 1969, carrying **Commander Neil Armstrong**, command module (CM) pilot **Michael Collins** and lunar module (LM) pilot **Edwin ('Buzz') Aldrin, Jr**. Four days, 13 hours and 42 minutes later – on **20 July 1969** – Armstrong stepped out and on to the surface of the Moon.

27. **1983**. Russian cosmonaut **Yuri Gagarin** became the first **man** in Space on 12 April 1961. Two years later, **Valentina Tereshkova** became the first **woman** in Space on 16 June 1963. But it was another 20 years before NASA put its first female astronaut – **Sally K. Ride** – in orbit.

28. **1971**. Astronauts **David Scott** and **James Irwin** landed on the Moon as part of the *Apollo 15* mission, taking a specially designed, battery-powered Lunar Rover buggy along for the ride. On

**30 July 1971**, they became the first people to drive not only off-road, but off-world.

29. **1997**. NASA's **Mars Pathfinder** probe landed on the surface of Mars on 4 July 1997, releasing a robotic rover (called the **Mars Sojourner**) that trundled about on its surface for almost three months, taking pictures and analysing rocks.

30. **1971**. The world's first space station – **Salyut 1** – was launched by the USSR (now Russia) on **19 April 1971**. It stayed in orbit for just six months, and was manned for just 23 days. The three-man crew of *Soyuz 11*, launched on 6 June, and docked with Salyut one day later. Three weeks later, they had to abandon the space station after an electrical fire, and transferred back to the *Soyuz* rocket to make the journey back to Earth.

The *Soyuz 11* capsule splashed down intact on 30 June, but when the recovery crew opened it they found that tragedy had struck. The cabin had depressurized during re-entry, and all three cosmonauts had died.

Two years later, NASA launched its first space station, Skylab. This one hosted three crews over a six-year period, before it was (intentionally) brought out of orbit. Skylab broke apart on re-entry, and the pieces splashed harmlessly into the ocean between South Africa and Australia.

B – **Ceres.** All these objects are officially recognized as dwarf planets. But while Eris, Pluto and Haumea all lie in outer solar system – beyond the orbit of the planet Neptune – Ceres lies in the *inner* solar system, between the planets Mars and Jupiter.

In fact, Ceres is the *only* (official) dwarf planet of the inner solar system. That may change in future, though, as many astronomers are arguing that the asteroids **Vesta** and **Pallas** are both large enough to be called dwarf planets too. Ceres, Vesta and Pallas all lie within the asteroid belt, just beyond Mars.

# E: MORE MEGA-BRAIN ANSWERS

**31. (a) star**

Like plants and animals, stars **live**, **die**, **develop** and **evolve**, and can be classified into **families** based on their physical features.

Our own star, the Sun, is a **class G yellow dwarf** star – making it fairly small, dim and cool compared with most other stars in the galaxy. Class G stars burn away at around 4,726–5,726°C, giving them a yellowish hue similar to molten steel.

Smaller, cooler, **class M** stars are less than half the size of our Sun, and simmer away at about 3,426°C. They have a reddish hue more like glowing coals or flowing lava, earning them the name **red dwarf**.

Further up the star scale, **class B blue giants** grow

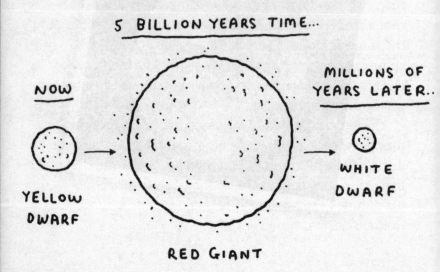

5 BILLION YEARS TIME...

NOW

MILLIONS OF YEARS LATER...

YELLOW DWARF

WHITE DWARF

RED GIANT

up to **16 times** the size of our puny, dwarf Sun, and burn up to **five times** hotter, at 9,726–29,726°C.

All these stars fall within the so-called **Main Sequence** of stars – which describes the most common types of star in the universe.

In fact, a single star will move *along* the Main Sequence as it ages, *evolving* from one star type into another in its journey from birth to death. Our own **yellow dwarf Sun**, for example, will swell into a **red giant** in about 5 billion years' time – becoming 200 times larger than it is now. Later still, it will burn off most of its mass and shrink to become a small, dense **white dwarf** star – the final state of being for smallish stars like our sun.

Other stars have different fates. **Blue giant** stars, far larger than our Sun, may end their lives in spectacular **supernova** explosions, leaving behind tiny, city-sized **neutron stars** so incredibly dense that a single *teaspoon* of its mass would weigh about the same as Mount Everest. Others become **pulsars** – spinning neutron stars that fling out regular pulses of electromagnetic radiation as they rotate, like strange, intergalactic lighthouses.

The very largest stars, **supergiants** and **hypergiants**, may grow over a million times larger than our own sun during their lifetimes. When *these* bad boys end their lives, they may collapse in on themselves to become **black holes** – super-dense invisible objects with an immense gravitational pull.

## 32. (b) barred spiral

Just as stars have classes and families, so too do galaxies.

In the 1930s, American astronomer **Edwin Hubble** (after whom the Hubble Space Telescope was named) spotted and named several galaxies outside our own, and began classifying them into types (or families), based on their general shape and appearance. Before this, most astronomers had believed that the Milky Way *was* the *entire universe*.

The three basic families Hubble pointed out were **elliptical galaxies**, **spiral galaxies** and **irregular galaxies**.

**Elliptical galaxies** are smooth, **ovoid** (egg-shaped) objects with stars spread out fairly evenly within. They can be further subdivided based on how large or how flat they are.

**Spiral galaxies** are spinning, disc-shaped objects that bulge in the middle, and have long, trailing 'arms' that spiral out from the centre. The arms are formed by large, bright stars held together by gravity, with smaller, dimmer stars forming the gaps in between. This group can be further divided into **spirals** and **barred spirals**. In barred spirals, the trailing arms seem attached to both ends of a long 'bar' of stars that runs through the middle of the central bulge.

Our own galaxy, the Milky Way, was long thought to be a spiral galaxy. But it has recently been reclassified as a **barred spiral**, after the NASA Spitzer Space Telescope (launched in August 2003) revealed that the Milky Way has a large, central bar of stars measuring

27,000 light-years from end to end. That's about a third of its total width (100,000 light-years).

**Irregular galaxies** describe everything that's not an elliptical or a spiral galaxy. The stars within them are bunched together, but seem randomly spaced. And their cloud-like, irregular shapes can make them tricky to spot.

Like stars, galaxies evolve and develop over time. Many exist in **clusters** that orbit each other. Galaxies may also sometimes **'eat'** each other when they drift too close, or sometimes **rip each other apart**.

### 33. (d)  it made it to the Moon, but failed to land
*Apollo 13* proved to be an unlucky mission for NASA astronauts Jim Lovell, Fred Haise and Jack Swigert, who nearly lost their lives flying to and from the Moon in April 1970.

*Apollo 13* was NASA's third manned mission to the Moon's surface, coming hot on the heels of the first successful Moon landing by *Apollo 11* in July 1969, and the equally successful *Apollo 12*, which landed four months later.

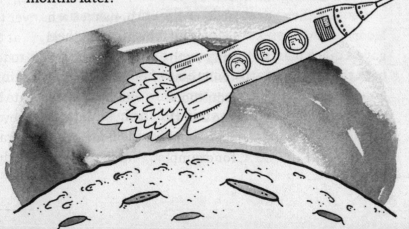

From the outset, the mission was beset with problems. A week before it launched, back-up pilot **Charles Duke** caught German measles, and exposed the whole crew (who had been living and training together for months) to infection. Fortunately, most of the others had already had the disease and were immune to it. All, that is, except for **Ken Mattingly**, the original Command Module pilot. Although he never actually contracted the disease, he was pulled off the crew at the last minute, putting back-up pilot Jack Swigert in his place.

Shortly after lift-off, one of the main rocket engines began to vibrate violently, and had to be shut down to avoid it shaking itself to pieces. Four outboard engines took over, and the craft barely made it into orbit.

Then, just over halfway to the Moon, last-minute substitute Swigert pushed a button to stir the spacecraft's oxygen tanks, and one of them promptly exploded, venting oxygen and fuel into space. They soon realized that they had no hope of landing on the Moon, and little hope of making it back alive, if they stuck to the original mission plan.

Instead, they powered down the craft, using the Moon's own gravity to swing round its far side, then gave a quick blast of the engines to send them hurtling back towards the Earth. Four hours before they entered the Earth's atmosphere, they abandoned the main service module and piled into the lunar landing module (LM), using it as a lifeboat for their descent to Earth.

Happily, the LM splashed down in the Pacific Ocean in one piece, and all three crew members were picked up by a US Navy aircraft carrier – shaken, disappointed, but alive and well.

*Apollo 13* was the only *Apollo* mission after 11 that didn't make it to the Moon. Makes you wonder whether they should have skipped straight to 14.

## 34. (c)  Gene Cernan

Pretty much everybody knows the name of the first man on the Moon, Neil Armstrong. And most, perhaps, could tell you the name of the second – 'Buzz' Aldrin. But few have heard of the last – Eugene A. Cernan, or 'Gene', to his mates.

Cernan was the commander of the final NASA lunar mission, *Apollo 17* – the other two crew members being pilots **Harrison H. Schmitt** and **Ronald E. Evans** – which launched on 7 December 1972, and returned to Earth twelve days later. It carried the first geologist in space (Schmitt), and part of its mission was to create a geological model of the Moon's crust and interior.

It also carried NASA's third **Lunar Rover** vehicle and, while Cernan wasn't the first astronaut to *drive* a car on the Moon, he was the first to *wreck* one. First, he snagged a discarded hammer and ripped a bumper off the Rover. Then he ran over some jagged rocks and dented its steel-mesh tyres.

Cernan and his crew left the Moon's surface around tea-time on 14 December 1972 and made it safely back to Earth. Since Cernan was the last one back into the Challenger lunar module when it left the Moon, he earned the rare (but less well-known) honour of being the **last** man on the Moon. At least for now!

## 35. (c) Search for Extra-Terrestrial Intelligence

**SETI** stands for the **Search for Extra-Terrestrial Intelligence**, and describes the effort to discover evidence of **alien life**, chiefly by looking for their radio signals.

Ever since SETI was first proposed in the 1960s, astronomers have been using radio telescopes to scan the skies – looking for strange signals or full-on transmissions from distant stars and galaxies.

This is no easy task. For starters, the sky is a pretty

SIGH... NOTHING!

SIGH... NOTHING!

*big* place, so the first task is to decide where you want to point your dish. Some have attempted to **scan the sky piece by piece**, focusing on one tiny slice of sky and moving the dish a fraction of a degree each night. Others have decided to **focus only on nearby systems**, reasoning that these are the only ones we have any hope of *reaching*, anyway.

The second major problem is computer power. Every day, SETI project telescopes produce millions of gigabytes of information. Analysing these signals requires *massive* amounts of processing power. To get around this, one project, run by the University of California at Berkeley, asks computer owners across the world to donate their spare computer power to analysing SETI data. Basically, you install a screensaver program that automatically downloads, analyses and uploads SETI data whenever your computer goes to into standby mode.

The project is called **SETI@home**, and if you want to sign up for it, go to **http://seti.berkeley.edu/setiathome/**

Fifty years on, SETI has yet to turn up any solid evidence of alien life. The closest yet was a mysterious signal (nicknamed the 'Wow!' signal) received by the Big Ear Observatory, Ohio, on 15 August 1977. The radio signal – which was thirty times more powerful than average deep-space background radiation – came from somewhere in the constellation of Sagittarius. It was never decoded or repeated, so we have no evidence that it was sent by an alien civilization. But it *could* have been.

## 36. (b) the event horizon

A black hole is a region of Space – usually one recently occupied by an imploding **supergiant** star – where matter collapses to a point of **infinite** density.

This is pretty hard for our human brains to imagine. Only **ÜberGeeks** like **Albert Einstein** and **Stephen Hawking** seem to be able to get the heads round it. Let's just say that the average black hole contains **ten times** as much mass as our **Sun**, but all that mass is squashed up into a point the size of a pinhead.

So, if black holes are that small, what's the problem? After all, you'd be hard-pressed to fall into a hole the size of a pinhead, right?

Well, here's the thing. The hole itself (or in technical terms, the **singularity**) might just be a tiny dot in Space. But the region of Space affected by its gravity is much, much larger. Close to the singularity, the fabric of space-time itself becomes so *warped* that **nothing** that enters could ever get out again. Beyond this 'point of no return', no star, no planet, no spacecraft – not even **light** – can escape. This is why black holes are invisible. This is also what makes them so dangerous.

In 1916, German astrophysicist **Kurt Schwarzschild** figured out a formula that tells us how wide this 'inescapable area' around a black hole will be, given its mass. This area forms a **sphere** in Space around the singularity. The distance from the *centre* of the black hole to the *edge* of that sphere is known as the **Schwarzschild radius**, and the outer boundaries of the sphere itself are called the **event horizon**.

For a black hole with a mass of ten suns, the Schwarzschild radius would be about **30 km** (or 19 miles), and the event horizon would be **60 km** (38 miles) wide. For practical purposes, this is how 'big' the black hole really is. Fly inside that 60 km-wide sphere and you'll never come out again. *Ever*.

Worse yet, you'll be frazzled by X-rays and ripped apart *incredibly slowly* by the immense electromagnetic and gravitational fields around the black hole.

So there you go. Black holes – *not* to be messed with.

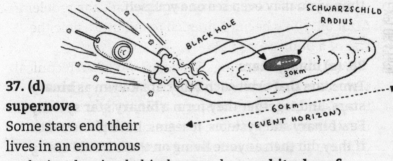

**37. (d) supernova**

Some stars end their lives in an enormous explosion, leaving behind super-dense **white dwarf** or **neutron stars.** The explosion is called a **supernova**, and when it happens a star can outshine a galaxy – releasing as much energy in one hour as our Sun would in its entire lifetime.

Only giant stars between **eight and twenty solar masses** 'go supernova'. When they do, the explosion itself is triggered in one of two ways:

- **Type I:** The star collects mass from another source (usually another star). When it reaches a certain size, it becomes like an enormous, unstable Jenga pile. Eventually, enough matter and pressure builds up to set off an immense nuclear super-explosion.

- **Type II:** The star burns off most of its mass (in other words, it runs out of fuel), and what's left behind collapses in on itself. Again, this produces a super-powerful nuclear explosion.

Supernovas happen within our galaxy (and others like it) about once every fifty years. If you're lucky – and you watch the right region of the sky, at the right time – you may even see one yourself.

## 38. (a) binary stars

Two stars that orbit each other are known as **binary stars**, and together they form a **binary star system**. Few binary star systems, it seems, have planets. But if they did then anyone living on them would see two suns rising and setting – sometimes together, sometimes not.

This 'twin star' arrangement is more common than you might think. In fact, astronomers reckon that *most* of the stars we see in the night sky are binary-star systems. Single-star systems (like ours) are a little rarer. In fact, if Jupiter were a hundred times bigger than it is, then it would have become a **star** rather than a planet. If that had happened, then instead of having **one star**, **eight planets** and (eventually) **intelligent life forms**, ours would have been a binary star system, with **two stars**, **no planets** and **no life** at all.

## 39. (b) the Andromeda Galaxy

The closest **spiral galaxy** to ours is the **Andromeda Galaxy**. It lies about **2.6 million light-years** from Earth, meaning that even if you could travel at the speed of light (which you can't) it would take over **2.6 million years** to get there.

Similarly, the light we see from the Andromeda Galaxy today left the stars within it over 2.6 million years ago, during the Palaeolithic Era on Earth. At that time, humans had yet to evolve, and our hairy, ape-like ancestors had just about figured out how to make tools from rocks and pebbles.

However, the Andromeda is **not** the *closest* galaxy to our own. There are at least 33 **elliptical** and **irregular dwarf** galaxies closer to us than Andromeda. In turn, these galaxies are part of a larger cluster of fifty or so galaxies astronomers call the **Local Group**.

## 40. (c) New General Catalogue

The **NGC** seen in the official names of stars and galaxies stands for **New General Catalogue**, indicating that they have been spotted, tracked and listed in the official international catalogue of celestial objects.

The first major catalogue was published in 1786 by planet, asteroid and comet spotter **William Herschel**. This listed about 1,000 stars and galaxies (although the galaxies were all identified as 'nebulae', as this is what astronomers called blurry star clusters before they knew what they were). He later added another 1,500 entries, and his son, John Herschel, added another 2,500, bringing the total number of stars and 'nebulae' in the updated *General Catalogue* (GC), published in 1864, to about 5,000.

The *New General Catalogue* (**NGC**) of stars was published in 1888. By that time, the list of celestial objects had grown to over **7,800**. Most of the extra ones were added by astronomer **John Louis Dreyer**.

The NGC is still the most complete list of stars and galaxies known today, even though it neglects many stars and galaxies visible in the southern hemisphere (Herschel and Dreyer both lived in the northern hemisphere, so couldn't see these). As such, astronomers still use it (albeit a computerized version) to identify and classify stars and galaxies. Whenever someone spots a new star or galaxy, they check first to see if it's in the NGC. If it is, then they can refer to its number (for example, NGC 224) in scientific papers, and everyone will know which one they're talking about, even without describing it, or giving its coordinates in the sky.

# ASTRO PUZZLER SOLUTION

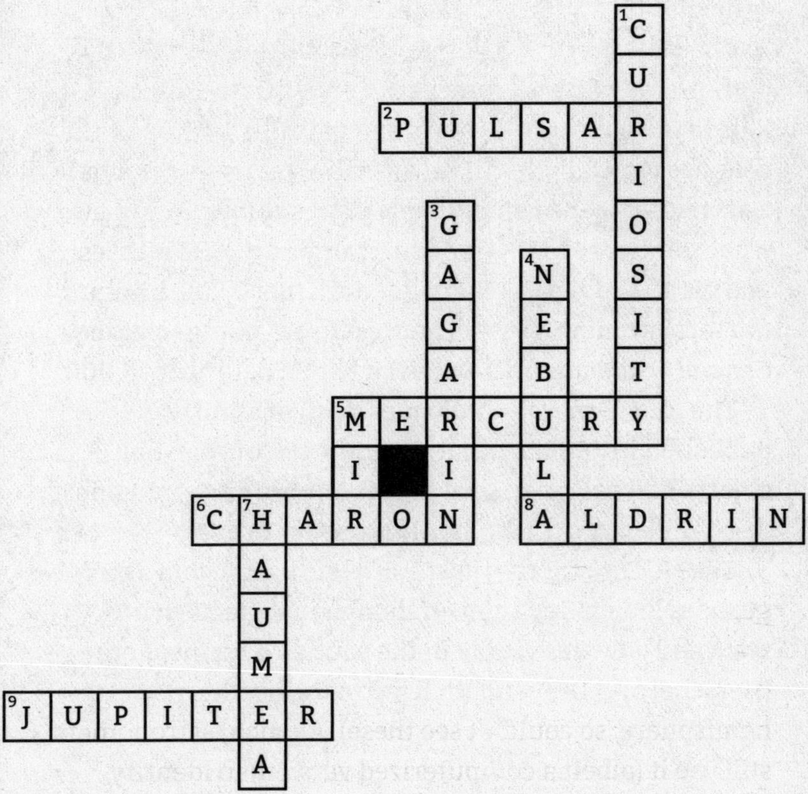

1 CURIOSITY
2 PULSAR
3 GAGARIN
4 NEBULA
5 MERCURY
5 MIR
6 CHARON
7 HAUMEA
8 ALDRIN
9 JUPITER

# ANSWERS

# PART TWO:
# BLOOD AND GUTS

# SUPERGEEK: ANSWERS

>>>>>>>>>>>>>>>>>>>>>>>>>>>>>>>>>>>
## A: MEGA-BRAIN ANSWERS

**1. (c) it helps you fight off infections**

For many years, doctors and anatomists (scientists who study the structure of the human body) couldn't figure out what the appendix was for. All it seemed to do was swell up and make you sick when it got infected, causing **appendicitis**. What's more, completely *removing* the tiny, sausage-like organ (as a cure for appendicitis) seemed to cause no ill effects.

People, it seemed, could survive just fine without an appendix. So most doctors decided that it must just be a useless, '**vestigial**' organ. 'Vestigial' means left over from an earlier time, when our plant-eating ancestors used it to store tough, leafy material to be digested later on. Many plant-eating animals still have

YOU KNOW, I'M NOT USELESS AFTER ALL!

>>>>>>>>>>>>>>>>>>>>>>>>>>>>>>>>>>>>>>>>>>>

one of these fleshy storage bags, otherwise known as a **caecum** ('see-kum'). But since we no longer eat tough leaves or grasses, the human caecum shrank until it became the useless, shrivelled sausage it is today.

However, if this were the case, then you'd expect the appendix of older apes and primates to be *larger* than ours: for example, bigger in a lemur than a chimp; and bigger in a chimp than a human. The trouble is they're not. The appendix of a chimp is even smaller than ours. And chimps still eat tough, woody foods.

As it turns out, the human appendix isn't useless at all. Instead of storing half-chewed grasses, it stores 'good' bacteria. When illness strikes, it can kill off the billions of helpful, harmless bugs that line the large intestines of a healthy person. If this happens, 'back-up' bacteria can move from their holding place in the appendix to replace them, crowding out the nasty, harmful bacteria that would otherwise sneak in.

The appendix, then, helps you to fight off future gut infections. That is, if you *have* one.

## 2. (a) connect muscles to bones

In school biology classes, we're usually told that our bony skeletons hold us up, and our muscles move our bones around. But this isn't quite true. In fact, muscles don't attach to bones *at all.* Rather, each muscle ends in a tough, fleshy strap called a **tendon**. It's *these* that attach the muscles to bones. (In fact, tendons don't attach directly to the bones, either. They attach to a network of fleshy, **fascial fibres** that surrounds bones, and pull through those. But that's another story.)

Tendons aren't as stretchy as muscles, but they can withstand a great deal of pulling before they rip and tear. This makes them ideal 'connectors'. Some tendons connect muscles to bones, while others connect muscles to other muscles. Tendons do not, however, connect one bone to another. That job is done by **ligaments**.

## 3. (c) 200–250 bones

Strange as it may seem, it's not easy to say *exactly* how many bones there are in the human body. A common figure seen in textbooks and on websites is **206**. But in reality it all depends on *how* you count them, and *when*.

At birth, babies have well over **300** individual bones, but, as the baby grows and develops, many of these fuse (join together) over time. The skull, for example, starts off in more than **20** pieces, including two **parietal bones** (which form the sides of the skull), the **occipital bone** (which forms the crown, or top of the skull), two **temporal bones** (which cover the temples) and the **frontal bone** (you guessed it – at the front of the head). By the time a baby starts to toddle, these bones will have fused into a single **cranium**.

By adulthood, the number of separate bones is **closer to 200 than 300**. But precisely how many there are depends on what you mean by 'separate'. Your foot, for example, contains **seven** individual bones, all clustered together, and your wrist consists of **eight**. So if someone tells you they've 'broken their foot' or 'broken their wrist', they could mean any one of the **30** bones (14 in the feet, 16 in the wrists) has been cracked. The various bones of the **pelvis** (hips), **sternum** (breastbone) and **ribcage** can also be counted in different ways. And some people have extra fingers or toes too!

Depending on how you count them, we can say that an adult might have anywhere between 200 and 250 bones in their body.

### 4. (d) 600–900 muscles

It's even harder to count muscles than to count bones. While bones fuse and merge over time, most muscles are permanently fused together already – bound into chains, bundles and sheets by the **fascia** (also known as **connective tissue**) that surrounds them.

All this makes it monumentally difficult to decide where one muscle ends and another begins. Some, like the biceps and triceps muscles of the upper arms, are pretty easy for surgeons and anatomists to separate out. Others, like the **erector spinae** muscles of the back, and the **serratus** muscles that wrap round the ribcage – are much harder to distinguish from their neighbours. Depending on how you look at them (or dissect them), you might end up with **one** muscle, or **twelve**.

And that's just the skeletal muscles that pull the bones and joints about. If you include all the **smooth muscle** in the body – including the ring of muscle at the base of every **hair follicle** on your body, then you have **over five million muscles**.

Limiting the count to the 'bone-moving' muscles alone, we can say that the average person has somewhere between 600 and 900 muscles in their body. It's worth noting, too, that weightlifters, bodybuilders and circus strongmen don't have any *more* muscles than anyone else. They just have *thicker* muscles that contain more muscle fibres, and have a better ability to *control* those muscle fibres using nerve impulses.

### 5. (c) A, B, O and AB

The four basic blood types in all human populations are A, B, O and AB. The groups are based on special proteins (called **antigens**) found on the surface of the bearer's red blood cells. These proteins come in one of two 'flavours' or types – A and B. Here's how it works:

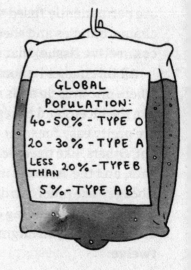

GLOBAL POPULATION:
40-50% - TYPE O
20 - 30% - TYPE A
LESS THAN 20% - TYPE B
5% - TYPE AB

• People with type 'A' proteins on their red blood cells have **Type A** blood.

- People with type 'B' proteins have **Type B** blood.
- People with both 'A' and 'B' proteins on their cells have **Type AB** blood.
- And people with neither 'A' nor 'B' proteins are **Type O**.

By far the most common group is Type O. Almost 50 per cent of the world's population is Type O. Another 20–30 per cent are Type A. In most places, Type B and AB are much rarer. (In India and a few other places, B is more common than A. But this is the exception, rather than the rule.)

So why do we bother separating people into these groups at all? Well, here's the thing. People with Type A blood also have **antibodies** that attack Type B antigens. So if you squirt Type B blood into a Type A person, the antibodies attack, causing the donated blood cells to stick together, forming a **lethal blood clot**.

Similarly, people with Type B blood have antibodies that attack Type A cells. So you can't give Type A blood to a Type B person either. Type AB people are lucky, as they have no such antibodies in their blood, and can accept blood from anyone. Type O people are unluckiest of all, as they have antibodies that attack both A and B antigens. So they can *only* receive blood from other Type O donors!

Confused yet? To make matters worse, you can divide the ABO groups further by looking for additional antigens called Rhesus proteins. People with type 'A' antigens *and* Rhesus proteins are called **Type A Rhesus**

**Positive** (or A+). The same person with no Rhesus proteins would be Type A Rhesus Negative (or A−).

Taking these into account, your blood type might be more fully described as O+, O−, A+, A−, B+, B−, AB+ or AB−!

## 6. (b) 30 centimetres (12 inches) long

As a general rule, your femur (or thigh bone) makes up a quarter, or 25 per cent, of your total height. More accurate ways of estimating height from bone length do exist. But if you want to avoid doing too many sums this isn't a bad approximation. Archaeologists use ratios like this to figure out how tall a person

would have been, just from looking at a single, unearthed femur bone. So if they found a 30 cm-long bone at some ancient Roman burial-site, they could quickly estimate that the owner was about 120 cm tall – most likely a child.

That said, proportions change with age, and are a little different between boys and girls. Adult males, for example, have humerus (or upper arm) bones that measure about one fifth of their total height. But using this [humerus X five = height] formula on the bones of a young girl wouldn't work so well. You'd end up thinking she was shorter than she actually was. Try measuring your own arm and leg bones, and see if it works for you!

### 7. (d) none of the above

While dust and cat hairs can all *trigger* asthma attacks, none of them can actually *give* you asthma in the first place.

Asthma is a disease of the respiratory system, which affects the lungs and airways. You don't 'catch' it as you would viral diseases like **influenza** or **Ebola**. And it isn't passed to us from animals, the way bacterial diseases like **toxoplasmosis** are.

Instead, asthma is caused by a malfunctioning immune system. A person with asthma has super-sensitive **immune cells** that attack pollen, cat hair or other harmless irritants that drift into the lungs as if they were deadly bacteria. The cells go crazy, pumping out a chemical called **histamine**, which in turn causes the lungs and airways to swell shut, making it harder and harder to breathe. So while dust and cat hair can trigger the allergic reaction of asthma, neither one made you allergic to them in the first place. In fact, many studies show that kids who grow up with cats and dust in the house are far *less* likely to suffer asthma attacks.

So what *does* cause asthma? To be honest, we're still

not certain. We know that genes play a part, so if your mother is asthmatic there's a good chance you will be too. But exposure to chemicals and air pollutants (particularly when you're still young, and the lungs have not fully developed) may play a part. Most likely, it's a little of both.

**8. (b) because their spines bend and shorten with age**
This happens for two main reasons. Firstly, as the years pass, decades of gravity pulling down on the spine causes the backbones (or vertebrae) to squash together, and the fluid-filled gaps between them to close up.

In fact, the spine 'shortens' this way every day of your life, making you roughly 1.25 cm shorter at the end of the day compared to when you first climbed out of bed. Each night, as you sleep, the spine lengthens out again, so that you're back to full height in the morning. But after several decades of squeezing, old folks may lose 2.5 cm or so as the spine eventually fails to bounce back.

Worse still, the spine not only squashes down under gravity, but if left unchecked, it also bends. Unless people exercise and stretch the spine regularly (which many old people fail to do), the spine's natural, 'S'-shaped curve can widen out, leaving the back arched, the shoulders hunched and the head hanging forward on the neck. This can take another 7.5 to 10 cm off a person's height, making them seem much shorter than they actually are.

## 9. (b) a few days

The length of time you can survive without water varies a lot, depending on where you are, how hot and dry it is, how fit you are and how efficiently your body processes water.

A trained soldier in a cool climate can survive without water for up to a **week**. But a tubby, unfit person in a desert can die of dehydration in less than **two hours**.

OTHER
STUFF

WATER

Your body is more than 70 per cent water, and your blood consists of more than 92 per cent water. Water is required for almost every chemical process that takes place in your body, including growth, repair, digestion, energy generation and sending signals to and from the brain. Fail to replace the water lost through sweat and urine, and your organs (notably your heart and brain) will begin to shut down.

## 10. (d) molar

Wisdom teeth, should you have them, are technically known as **third molars**.

> Molars are, of course, the flat-crowned grinding teeth at the back of your mouth, used for chewing up tough food morsels.

A full, healthy mouth features at least **eight molars**, along with **eight premolars**, **four canines**, and **eight incisors**. Wisdom teeth are something of a bonus. A third set of four molars that appears behind the others, typically between 17 and 25 years of age.

Some people, though, *never* develop wisdom teeth. Or rather the wisdom teeth develop, but remain within their upper and lower jawbones for life, never bothering to erupt through the gum-line. This is fine. We can manage just fine without them. In fact, *having* wisdom teeth can be a real pain, as when they do emerge they often press painfully against the other molars, causing toothaches, infections and other problems.

So why do we have them at all? Well, wisdom teeth are a hangover from an earlier evolutionary time when we chewed more tough, woody plants and we *needed* more molars to grind it all down.

# B: PICTURE PUZZLE 1

## What is it?

A – **heart**

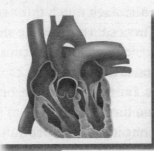

B – **kidney**

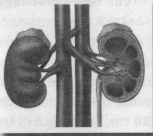

C – **liver**

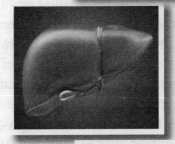

D – **spleen**

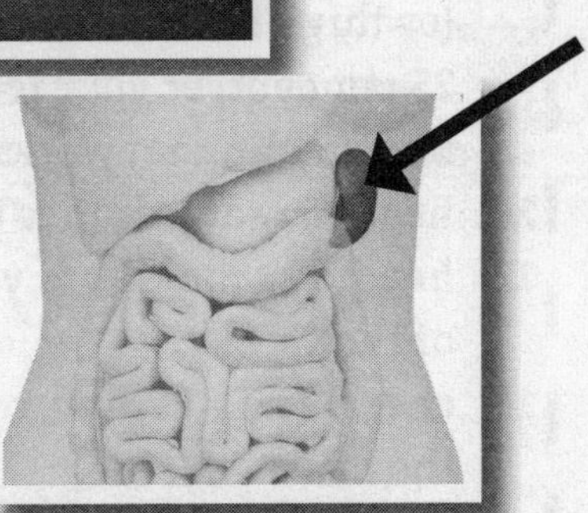

113

# C: QUICK-FIRE ANSWERS

11. **7 metres**. Although much *thinner* than your large intestine (hence its name), the small intestine is actually *far longer*. This is because it's where most of your food is digested and absorbed.

12. **1.5 metres**. The large intestine, or **colon**, traces a path around the coiled bundle of the small intestine, doing just one lap of the abdominal cavity.

13. **30 cm**. Your **oesophagus**, or food tube, runs from the back of your throat to the upper opening of your stomach. Depending on how tall you are, that distance could stretch anywhere from 20 cm to 40 cm or more. For an adult male of average height, it measures around 30 cm long.

14. **30 cm**. The length of the **humerus**, or upper arm bone, also varies with height and body shape. But a good rule of thumb is that the humerus will be a little under a fifth (or 20 per cent) as long as a person is tall. For an adult male of average height, that works out at around **30–35 cm**.

15. **50 cm**. Another good rule of thumb is that **femurs** (or thigh bones) make up about a quarter (or 25 per cent) of your total height. For the average male adult, that works out at about 40–50 cm long.

16. **head**. The **cranium** is the upper part of the skull.

17. **head**. The **maxilla** is your upper jaw bone, also part of the skull.

18. **chest**. The **sternum**, or breastbone, sits in front of the heart.

19. **leg**. The **fibula** is the smaller of the two bones in your lower leg, or shin.
20. **arm**. The **ulna** is one of the two bones in your forearm, the other being the **radius**.
21. **lung**. **Pulmonary** diseases like asthma, pneumonia and tuberculosis all affect the lungs and airways.
22. **heart**. **Cardiac arrest** is the medical name for a heart-stoppage, or heart attack.
23. **liver**. **Hepatic** means 'to do with the liver'. The liver is supplied with blood by the **hepatic artery**, and a liver infection is called **hepatitis**.
24. **kidney**. **Renal** means 'of the kidneys' – the main organs of the body's excretory system. Each kidney is supplied with blood by a **renal artery**. Inside, the blood is 'cleaned' as it passes through a network of filtering membranes. This removes waste products from the blood, and passes them to the bladder to be squirted out of the body in the form of **urine**.
25. **heart**. The heart is a powerful, fleshy pump made of cardiac muscle, arranged into four chambers. Blood arrives at the heart via the two entrance chambers or **atria**, and pumped out of the two **ventricles** below.
26. **arms**. Your **biceps brachii** (or just 'biceps' for short) are the muscles on the inside of each upper arm.
27. **legs**. **Biceps femoralis** is another name for your **hamstring** muscles, which run down the back of each thigh. Contracting a hamstring bends your leg at the knee.
28. **stomach**. The **abdominal** muscles (or 'abs' for

short) protect the delicate organs of the belly, and are tightened when you curl into a ball or bend your spine forward.

29. **chest**. Your **pectoral muscles** (or 'pecs') run from the shoulders to the breastbone, or **sternum**. They are powerful muscles used for pushing and pressing.

30. **legs**. Your **quadriceps** (or 'quads') are the huge muscles at the front of each thigh. Contracting them straightens your leg at the knee, or pushes you up out of a squat.

# D: PICTURE PUZZLE 2

**Odd one out**

A – **Lungs** are the odd ones out here.

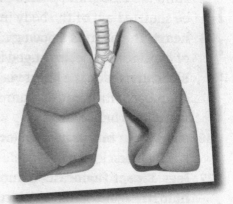

The other organs and bones (the **teeth**, **intestines** and **stomach**) are all part of the **digestive** system, while the lungs are part of the **respiratory** system.

# E: MORE MEGA-BRAIN ANSWERS

**31. (d) gluteus maximus**

Believe it or not, the largest muscle in your body is in your bottom! Your weighty **gluteus maximus** muscles stretch across the back of your hips – from your tailbone to the outside of each hip – creating the classic, rounded contours of your 'bum cheeks'. Even in people without much of a 'bum', the gluteus maximus muscles (or 'glutes', as bodybuilders call them) are the largest and heaviest in the body.

So why do we need such powerful bum muscles? Surely it's not just padding, so that we always have something comfortable to sit on?

Actually, it's more to do with *standing* and *walking* than sitting. If you think about it, when you're standing up straight, the whole of the upper body – head, chest, arms, belly, the lot – is balanced on top of your hips. The hips, of course, are supported from below by the twin pillars of your legs. Your back muscles and abdominal muscles keep your spine and torso upright when you walk or stand, but without powerful bum muscles to keep your hips in the right position your body would buckle in the middle, and you'd collapse.

This is exactly what happens when toddlers first learn to stand and walk. Using a chair or other object for support, most toddlers quickly figure out how to pull themselves up to their feet. But when they try to stand or walk without support, it's their *hips* that

buckle, not their knees. When they
*do* start walking, they toddle
about with their bum sticking
out backwards. It's only later
that they learn to engage their bum
muscles fully, and pull the hips under
the torso using their powerful glutes.

## 32. (d) all of the above

The liver is the ultimate multi-tasking organ. The heart
pumps blood. The lungs pump air. The intestines digest
food. But the liver does *many* different things.

Like the kidneys, it **filters blood** to remove waste
products. But it also digests and removes a good
number of **poisons** and **toxins**, turning them into
harmless chemicals that the body can use or excrete.

The liver (along with the gall bladder that lies
beneath it) helps us to **break down fats**, turning them
into useful energy, or storing them as fatty acids. The
liver also **stores the essential vitamins and minerals**
we get from our food, keeping them in reserve for
leaner times. It does this job so well that, with a well-
balanced diet, the average person has enough vitamin
A and B12 stored in their liver to last for a **year** or more.

Perhaps its most important job is controlling the
supply of **energy** to the body. It does this by producing
and storing **glucose** – the main energy source used by
your muscles, and the *only* one used by your brain.

The downside to having such a versatile,

multitasking liver is that you can't live long without it. When too much of a poison (including alcohol) is taken in too quickly, the liver can stop working completely, and none of these jobs get done. The only hope then is a **liver transplant** – which tends to be much trickier than a heart or kidney transplant.

### 33. (b) pancreas

While the trachea, diaphragm and bronchi are all part of your body's breathing (or respiratory) system, the **pancreas** is not. It's part of your digestive system – producing **enzymes** that help your body to digest fats, proteins and sugars.

Your **trachea**, more commonly known as your *windpipe*, runs from the back of your throat to the middle of your chest. It forms the entryway for oxygen moving into your respiratory system, and the exit route for carbon dioxide moving out. The trachea ends in an upside-down Y-junction, splitting into two large tubes

TRACHEA

BRONCHIOLES

ALVEOLI

BRONCHI

DIAPHRAGM

called **bronchi**, which in turn split into smaller air tubes called **bronchioles**.

These branches eventually end at little berry-like structures called **alveoli**, which are filled with fluid and covered with tiny blood vessels. Here, oxygen and carbon dioxide dissolve in and out of the bloodstream. The oxygen passes in, to be carried away by red blood cells, while the carbon dioxide passes out, to be breathed back out through the bronchioles, bronchi and trachea.

None of this, though, would be possible without the rhythmic pull and push of the **diaphragm** – a curving, sheet-like muscle that lies beneath the lungs. When the diaphragm is contracted, it pulls itself downwards, creating space for the lungs to inflate. As it relaxes, the intestines and other organs below push it back upwards, and air is squeezed back out of the lungs, like a bellows.

### 34. (d) blood

**Anaemia**, **thalassaemia** and **haemophilia** are all diseases of the blood. They are all **genetic** diseases, meaning that you're *born* with them, rather than catching them later in life.

People with **anaemia** lack enough healthy red blood cells to carry all the oxygen they need. Some anaemia sufferers simply don't make *enough* red blood cells. Others make blood cells that don't bind and carry oxygen as well as they should.

**Thalassaemia** is a similar kind of blood disease.

People with thalassaemia have plenty of red blood cells, but the **haemoglobin** molecules inside are misshapen, meaning that they cannot bind and carry molecules of oxygen as efficiently as those of a healthy person.

**Haemophilia** is a different type of blood disease. It prevents the blood from **clotting** properly (or in some cases, at all). Ordinarily, blood clots are formed by **platelets** and **clotting factors** in the blood. When you're cut, your platelets and clotting factors trigger a cascade of chemical reactions that eventually build a tough, sticky clot, made from a protein called **fibrin**. This stops too much blood from flowing out at the wound site.

But people with **haemophilia** are born with missing or malfunctioning clotting factors. So the chain of reactions is not completed, and the blood fails to clot entirely, fails to clot properly or fails to clot quickly enough to be useful.

**35. (d) in your hands and feet**
**Phalanges** are the bones of your fingers and toes. At the base of each hand is the **carpus** – a cluster of eight **carpal bones** that attach to the bone of the forearm to form the wrist joint. Beyond that lie the five **metacarpal** bones, which fan out to create the flat structure of the hand. Next come the **proximal phalanges**, which form the first joint of each finger. Next come the **intermediate phalanges** (middle finger joints), and finally the **distal phalanges** (fingertip joints).

The arrangement of bones in the foot is very similar (which is not so surprising, if you realize that hands evolved from feet). The base of the foot (including those of the heel and ankle) is made up of a seven-bone cluster called the **tarsus**. In front of that lie five **metatarsals**, which form the instep (the bit you kick a football with). Each metatarsal is tipped with its own set of **proximal**, **intermediate** and **distal phalanges**.

## 36. (b) white blood cell

**Red** blood cells carry oxygen. **Platelets** trigger blood clots. **Blue** blood cells don't exist (sorry, Your Majesty). But it's **white** blood cells (or **leucocytes**) that fight off bacteria and viruses.

White blood cells form the vanguard (the front line of defence) of your body's **immune system**, which keeps your blood and organs free (or immune) from disease. There are several types of white blood cell, all with important defensive roles.

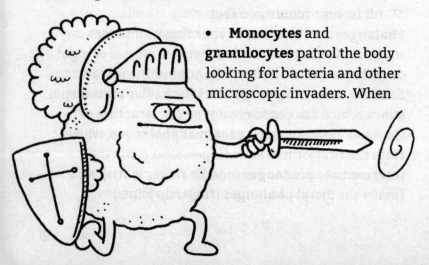

- **Monocytes** and **granulocytes** patrol the body looking for bacteria and other microscopic invaders. When they find them, they *engulf* the invader and *digest* it using powerful enzymes.

- **B lymphocytes** produce antibodies – proteins that bind to the outer shells of bacteria and viruses, surrounding them and marking them for destruction.
- **T lymphocytes** cluster around cells infected by bacteria or viruses, and multiply to create an army of reinforcements.

Some lymphocytes are assassins, which destroy infected cells outright, to stop the infection spreading to neighbouring cells. And some remain in the bloodstream for many years after an infection, ready to fight off any future attack by the same organism. It's these 'memory' cells and their antibodies that make you **immune** to diseases you caught once before.

## 37. (c) coccyx
The **scapula**, **humerus** and **clavicle** are all part of your shoulder joint. That makes the **coccyx** (or tailbone) the odd one out.

Your **scapula** is better known as your **shoulder blade**. You have two **scapulae** which sit outside the ribcage and float around your upper back. Each scapula forms an anchor for muscles that attach to the **humerus** – the bone inside your upper arm. The scapula acts as a counterweight to the arm, moving downward as the arm raises up, and vice versa.

Your **clavicles**, better known as **collarbones**, run from the front of each shoulder to the top of the breastbone. These anchor the shoulder blades to the breastbone, and support the structure of the shoulder as it rotates. Clavicles are thin and easily broken. They're commonly fractured when people fall and stick an arm out to save themselves. If the arm is kept stiff during a fall like this, the shockwave caused by the impact will travel right up the arm and snap the collarbone in two.

Ouch!

**38. (d) viruses and bacteria**
**Vaccines** are actually made using the bacteria or viruses that cause disease. The idea is to expose your body's immune cells to nasty bugs in advance, so that they have a chance to recognize the attacker, mount an effective defence and create memory cells and antibodies that will leave you immune to that particular bacterium or virus for the future.

Of course, you can't just go about injecting

dangerous microbes into

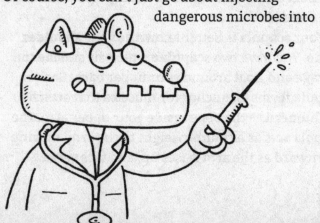

people, hoping they'll survive. Instead, safe vaccines are created by removing the dangerous bits of a microbe (the bits that allow them to multiply and infect cells), and injecting only the safe parts. **Live vaccines** consist of whole bacteria and viruses that are harmless or altered to make them safe. **Killed vaccines** consist of dead virus parts (usually just the outer coat proteins) that trigger a safe, useful immune response all by themselves.

Thanks to vaccines, **polio** and **smallpox** have been pretty much wiped out in the developed world, and far fewer children die of whooping cough, measles, mumps and rubella.

## 39. (c) ear wax

**Cerumen** is the technical, medical name for ear wax. It's made from a fatty, gooey substance squeezed out of glands inside the ear canal – the same kind that squeeze sweat on to the surface of the skin. Cerumen, however, is quite different to sweat. In addition to water and oily fats, it also contains dead skin cells, rotten ear hairs and more than a few dead bacteria. The function of ear wax is to protect the delicate ear drum from dust, dirt and infection by bacteria. For the most part, it does this very well, but

OUTER EAR

CERUMEN

EAR DRUM

if too much ear wax builds up in the ears it can block off the eardrum (causing temporary hearing loss) and trap bacteria *inside* the ear canal instead, leading to painful ear infections. For this reason, doctors may sometimes break up clotted ear wax with a blast of warm water from a syringe. While this does the job nicely, it also sounds like a massive waterfall rumbling into your head.

**40. (b) TB (tuberculosis)**
**Measles** is caused by the *Rubeola* virus, **Ebola** by the *Ebola* virus. And **influenza** by (you guessed it) the *Influenza* virus. **Tuberculosis** (or **TB**), on the other hand, is caused by a type of bacterium, called *Mycobacterium tuberculosis*.

The TB bacterium is a particularly nasty one, which is spread by inhaling the sneeze or cough droplets of an infected person. Once inside the body, it infects the lungs and destroys the delicate tissues within, leaving you unable to breathe properly. Worse yet, it can spread from the lungs to your bones and brain, causing irreversible damage, or even death. *Mycobacterium tuberculosis* is a very common bacterium, and TB is a very common disease, especially in Third World countries. It's estimated that over two billion people currently have the disease, and millions die from it each year.

This is why in the UK we vaccinate all schoolchildren against TB, between the ages of 10 and 14.

# BODY PUZZLER SOLUTION

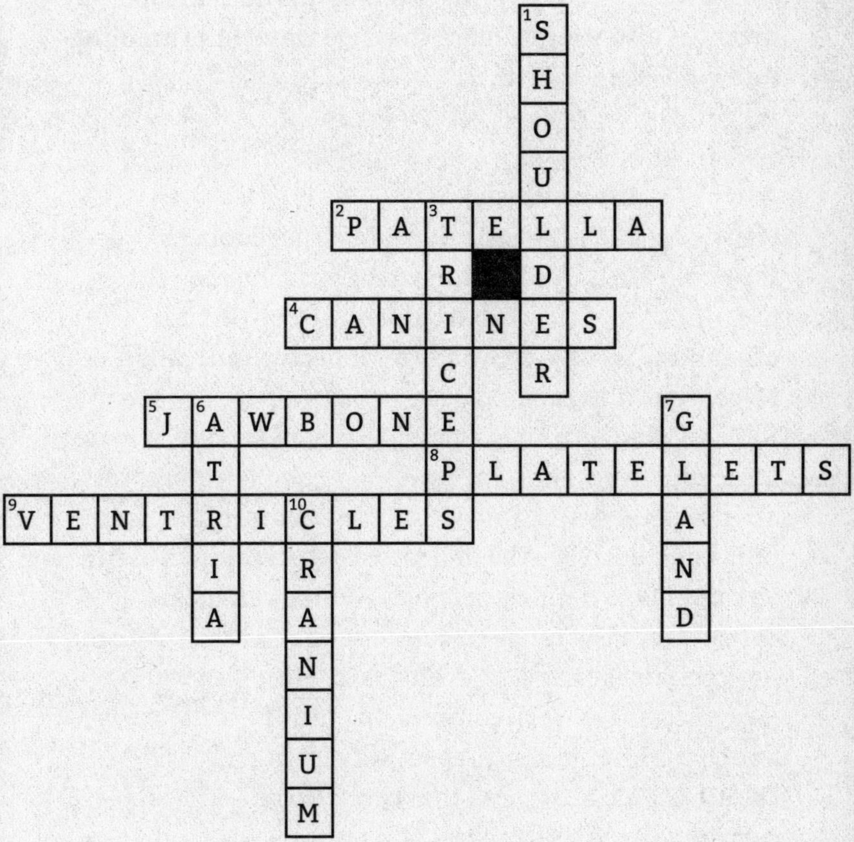
1 SHOULDER
2 PATELLA
3 TRICEPS
4 CANINES
5 JAWBONE
6 ATRIA
7 GLAND
8 PLATELETS
9 VENTRICLES
10 CRANIUM

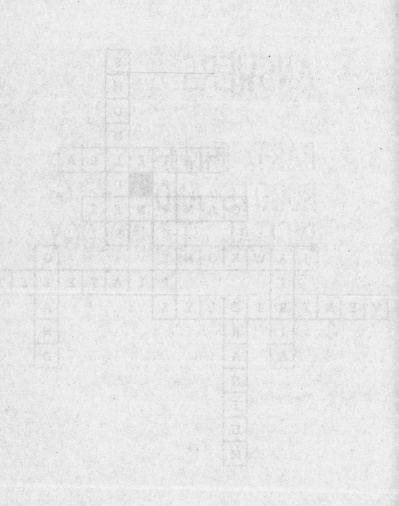

# ANSWERS

# PART THREE: ROBOTS AND DIGITAL TECHNOLOGY

# SUPERGEEK: ANSWERS
>>>>>>>>>>>>>>>>>>>>>>>>>>>>>>>
## A: MEGA-BRAIN ANSWERS

**1. (b) Charles Babbage**

The first calculating machine was invented by German mathematician **Wilhelm Schickard** in **1623**. Built of wood and brass, it used six rotating cylinders marked with numbers – along with a host of wheels, gears and dials – to calculate **logarithms** (complex multiplications that are hard for people to do in their heads, or even on paper).

French mathematician and philosopher **Blaise Pascal** built a similar device in **1642**. While neither machine really qualifies as 'the first computer', they were important because they showed people that machines could do things like addition and multiplication of which only *human brains* were thought capable.

The prize for inventing the first **mechanical computer** (as opposed to a calculator) goes to British engineer and mathematician **Charles Babbage**. In **1820**, he began work on his '**Difference Engine**', which could do complex arithmetic sums with answers correct to 19 decimal places. Halfway through building this incredibly complex machine (it required over 25,000 precision-crafted parts), Babbage gave up on it and began planning his next masterpiece – an '**Analytical Engine**' that could actually solve equations.

>>>>>>>>>>>>>>>>>>>>>>>>>>>>>>>>>>>>>>>>>>>

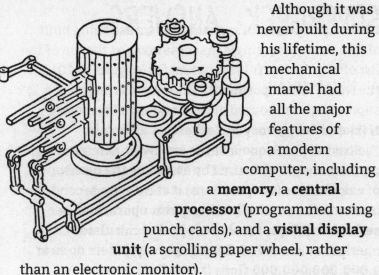

Although it was never built during his lifetime, this mechanical marvel had all the major features of a modern computer, including a **memory**, a **central processor** (programmed using punch cards), and a **visual display unit** (a scrolling paper wheel, rather than an electronic monitor).

## 2. (c) 1,000,000,000 (1 billion) bytes

A *byte* is a unit of digital information, and the size of a computer's memory is determined by the number of bytes it can store. Early digital computers could only store a few thousand bytes' worth of information. But within a few years, they could hold a *million* bytes or more. Just as long distances are measured in **kilometres**, rather than **metres**, the massive storage capacity of a modern computer is measured in **kilobytes**, **megabytes**, and even larger units. Here's how it works:

- 1 **kilobyte** (kB) = **1,000** bytes
- 1 **megabyte** (MB) = 1,000 **kB**, or 1 **million** bytes
- 1 **gigabyte** (GB) = 1,000 **MB**, or 1 **billion** bytes
- 1 **terabyte** (TB) = 1,000 **GB**, or 1 **trillion** bytes

## 3. (b) USA

New, super-powerful *supercomputers* are being built all the time, so no single machine stays at the top of the list of most powerful computers for long. As of 2012, the world's most powerful computer was **Sequoia**, a supercomputer housed at the **Lawrence Livermore National Laboratory** in **Berkeley, California**.

So what put Sequoia at the top? Well, computer performance is measured by assessing the number of calculations (or operations) it can do in a second, otherwise known as **floating-point operations per second** – or **flops**, for short. A pocket calculator operates at around 10 flops. Supercomputers do so at **1,000,000,000,000 flops (1 teraflop)** or more.

Sequoia operates at around **16.2 petaflops** (equal to 16,200,000,000,000,000 flops, or 16,200 teraflops). That makes it about **200,000 times** more powerful than the average MacBook Pro laptop, and **a quadrillion times** more powerful than a pocket calculator.

## 4. (a) about 2 kilobytes

Incredibly, the Apollo 11 Guidance Computer (AGC) worked with less 2 kilobytes of Random Access Memory (RAM), and 32 kilobytes of Read-Only Memory (ROM).

Now, compare that with a modern laptop, like the **MacBook Air** I am currently using to write this book. It has **2GB** of RAM – over a **million times** more memory than the computer that took three men to the Moon! At 2 GHz, my swanky new laptop also runs around a

million times *faster* than the AGC.

Just think about that. A rocket over 30 metres tall, containing over 3,000 tonnes of explosive fuel, travelling at over 26,000 mph, making a round trip of close to 100,000 miles. All controlled by something with less memory and processing power than an early model iPod.

## 5. (a) Removing errors from a program

In **engineering speak**, a *bug* is problem, defect or error with a machine, which needs to be fixed before it can resume its normal function. The process of figuring out what the problem is, and fixing it, is called 'removing the bugs' or 'de-bugging'.

So to **computer programmers** a *bug* is a defect in a software program, which has to be located and fixed (*de-bugged*) before the program will run.

There's a well-known story that the phrase 'de-bugging' dates back to the early 1940s, when American engineers at Harvard University were testing one of the first multipurpose computers – the Mark II. The story goes like this: the Mark II stopped working, and they couldn't figure out why. When they finally got around to opening up the panels of the (room-sized) machine, they found **actual bugs** (electrocuted moths) inside. To fix it, they had to remove the bugs.

In reality, however, engineers had actually been using the terms *bug* and *de-bug* for more than a **century** before the Mark II – or any other electronic computer – came along.

This use of the word *bug* probably comes from the ancient German word *bogge,* or the Scottish word *bogill* – both of which mean *goblin* or *gremlin*.

## 6. (b) TRICKY

**BASIC**, **JAVA** and **PYTHON** are all real computer languages. But while *learning* one can be tricky there isn't actually a computer language called **TRICKY**.

Computers, unlike people, do not understand spoken human languages (at least not yet). Nor can they use them to talk to each other. Instead, they use number-based codes to make sense of the world. So in order to 'talk' to computers, programmers have to translate their messages and instructions into code first.

In the earliest days of computing, this meant tapping in numbers, one after the other, or punching holes in cards to represent number patterns and sequences. Later, programmers created artificial languages that allowed them to translate whole ideas and functions into computer code, and make their instructions more powerful and precise.

## 7. (b) Mole

In computer terms, a virus is a computer program that copies itself and spreads from one computer to another. Some viruses are harmless, while others are extremely harmful.

The most common type of virus is the **worm**. Worms are programs that copy themselves over and over, spreading between the memory drives of a single computer, or between distant computers (often via e-mail). Harmful worms may carry instructions to delete files or send copies of your files back to a central database.

**Trojan horses** are another common virus type. Just as the legendary hollow Trojan horse helped murderous soldiers sneak into the ancient city of Troy, Trojans (for short) hide within software programs that are passed off as helpful or useful. When the user downloads and installs the new software, the Trojan sneaks out and installs itself too.

**Bootsector** viruses install themselves in the 'bootstrapping' section of a hard disk, which is accessed every time you switch on your computer.

These are particularly hard to spot and get rid of, but (thankfully) rarer than most other virus types.

Other types include **Rootkit** viruses (which give control of your computer to someone else, via the Internet), **Polymorphic** viruses (which continually change form, making them almost impossible to spot) and **Time Bombs** (which can lie dormant for years, then 'go off' at a certain date and time – deleting files or destroying software).

### 8. (d) Deep Blue

Chess is a game of probabilities and calculated risks. That said, the number of possible chess games is said to be more than the number of stars in our visible universe.

The first chess-playing computer program was written in **1958**, by programmer Alex Bernstein. It beat a few beginners and amateurs, but was soundly trounced – over and over again – by the professionals. At that time, leading computer scientists reckoned it would be just ten years before someone developed a program that could beat a human Chess Grandmaster. In reality, it took a lot longer than that.

By 1974, advanced chess computers were playing each other in computer chess world championship tournaments. By 1989, IBM's Deep Thought had become the world (computer) champion. But still no computer had ever bested a human Grandmaster. World (human) champion and Grandmaster Garry Kasparov played Deep Thought later that same year, and *thrashed* it.

In 1996, after seven years of development, Deep Thought was renamed **Deep Blue**, and it played Kasparov again. Once again, it lost. But not by much! For the next five months, a team of human grandmasters taught Deep Blue how to win from every possible end-game position they could think of. And when it met Kasparov again in 1997, the computer finally **won**.

## 9. (b) the Turing Test

The idea of **Artificial Intelligence** (**AI**) – or machines that show real, human-like intelligence – has been around since the early 1940s. But no computer yet has managed to pass the standard exam for true AI – the **Turing Test**.

The idea for the Turing Test – developed by

pioneering British computer scientist Alan Turing –
is quite simple. If a computer can fool an intelligent
human into thinking it is human, then it can be said to
be intelligent too.

The basic test looks like this: a human volunteer
(H1) sits in one room in front of a computer, ready
for some IM chat. In a second room sits another chat-
ready human subject (H2). In a third room, there is a
computer (C), linked to the same chat thread.

H1 doesn't know whether the other two chatters

are human or not. So he/she starts chatting, asking
questions that he thinks a computer and a real person
would answer differently. After a set time (say, five
minutes chatting to each), H1 is asked to identify which
(if any) of the other two chatters are computers. If H1
cannot tell the difference between the human and
computer-generated responses, then C is said to be
Artificially Intelligent.

A couple of programs (known as chatterbots) have passed short versions of the Turing Test – prompting computer scientists to say that the test doesn't work. But to date, no computer has managed to fool a human subject for longer than twenty minutes.

## 10. (d) Iceland

Although **China** has the highest number of Internet users (over half a billion, at the last count), **Iceland** has the highest *percentage* of Internet users. In a country of just **311,000** people, over **304,000** use the Internet. That's almost **98 per cent** of the population!

**Norway** has the second-greatest proportion of Internet users. Around **96 per cent** of Norwegians (**4.6 million** in a total population of around **4.7 million**) are regular Internet users. **Sweden** (93 per cent), and **Denmark** (89 per cent) aren't far behind.

By comparison, only **78 per cent** of Americans are Internet users, and just **38 per cent** of Chinese people. Being far larger in area, wide areas of China and North America still remain untouched by the Internet. Even in areas with cables and connections, the huge gap between the rich and poor means that many people cannot afford a computer, let alone an Internet connection. But in Scandinavian countries, the land area, the population and the gap between the rich and poor are all smaller. So the Internet is *everywhere*.

# B: PICTURE PUZZLE 1

**What is it?**

A – **HDD** (Hard Disk Drive)

B – **USB** (Universal Serial Bus) Port

C – **VGA** (Video Graphics Array) Port

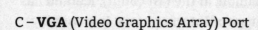

D – **CPU** (Central Processing Unit)

# C: QUICK-FIRE ANSWERS

11. **1978**. The idea of the cellular (or mobile-phone) network goes right back to 1947, but the technology needed to create one didn't arrive until the 1970s. The first experimental mobile phone call was placed in 1973, inside AT&T's Bell Labs in New Jersey, USA.

12. **1951**. The first colour TV programme was aired in **June 1951**, by the American CBS television network. Since hardly anyone had a colour TV, less than 1,000 people saw it in their own homes.

13. **1971**. American computer engineer Ray Tomlinson created the programming code for email addresses (along with the '@' symbol) in 1971, and used it to

send the world's first email – via the pre-Internet ARPANet system. Apparently, it read 'QWERTYUIOP'. Yes, that's right. On this historic occasion, he just hit all the letters on the top row of the keyboard.

14. **1971**. The world's first microprocessor chip, the **Intel 4004**, was built by **Robert Noyce**, founder of the **Intel** company, in **1971**.

15. **1977**. The world's first interlinked computer network (or inter-net) was built by the US military's Advanced Research Projects Agency (ARPA) in 1969. It linked computers in three university computer labs – three of them in California, and one two states away at the University of Utah. They christened it **ARPANet**. But the world's first **global Internet** (the ancestor of today's World Wide Web) didn't arrive until **1977**, when programmers Vint Cerf and Robert Kahn successfully linked three networks in San Francisco, London and Virginia.

16. **USA**. In **1947**, engineer **Thomas Goldsmith** created a very basic computer game – which simulated missiles arcing toward target shapes – using a cathode-ray TV screen. Then in **1958** **William Higinbotham** created the game *Tennis for Two* – which pinged a small dot back and forth between two T-shaped bats – using the screen of an oscilloscope. In **1961**, three students at the Massachusetts Institute of Technology (MIT) created a digital shoot-'em-up called *Spacewar!* using a programmable mini-computer and digital

display screen. *Any* of these could lay claim to being the first 'proper' video game. In any case – since they were all created at American universities, by American programmers – it's safe to say that the **USA** gave us the first video game.

17. **Japan**. The first realistic, functional android was unveiled by designer (and professor of robotics at Osaka University) **Hiroshi Ishiguro** in **2003**. Called **Actroid**, the robot resembled a life-size Japanese woman, complete with skin, hair and realistic facial features.

18. **UK**. Electronic television pioneer **John Logie Baird** and telephone inventor **Alexander Graham Bell** were both from **Scotland** (although Bell moved to the United States before building the first phone).

19. **Japan**. CDs and DVDs were both invented by engineers at Japan's **Sony** corporation (although Dutch company **Phillips** were also heavily involved in their development).

20. **Other**. **Israel** lays claim to inventing the first USB flash memory drive. The **Disk-On-Key** flash drive, built by Israeli company **M-Systems**, went on sale in December 2000, with an 8 MB memory capacity – more than **five times** that of the floppy disks used at that time. Rival companies in Singapore and China also claim to have invented flash drives at around the same time. So they're either an Asian or a Middle-Eastern invention.

21. **2001**. The first Apple iPod went on sale in **November 2001**. It wasn't the first digital audio

player invented. Korean electronics company SaeHan had released their portable, digital music player four years earlier. And other rival companies made their own, competing versions. But the iPod blew them all out of the water. Over **300 million** iPods have now been sold worldwide.

22. **1991**. British computer programmer **Tim Berners-Lee**, a researcher at the CERN particle physics lab in Switzerland, invented the first **web browser program** in 1991, turning an exclusive and tricky-to-use Internet into the easily searched World Wide Web system we know and love today. Perhaps most importantly, Berners-Lee invented the **hypertext (http)** protocol used to link web pages, and the **URL** (http://www . . .) addresses we use to label and navigate to them.

23. **1988**. The first **digital electronic cameras** were invented in Japan, and didn't arrive until the late 1980s. The first was the **Fuji DS-1P**, which went on sale in **1988**.

24. **1991**. CDs were first invented in 1982, but it took more than a decade for them to *really* catch on. By 1988, CDs were outselling the easily scratched vinyl records that had been around for a hundred years. But despite their far better sound quality, CDs didn't start outselling cassette tapes until **1991**.

25. **1983**. The first official laptop computer (or at least the first to *call* itself a 'laptop') was the **Gavilan SC**, which went on sale in **May 1983**. It weighed four kilograms (nine pounds), cost around

£2,000 and had just 48 kb of memory.

26. **Asia**.  As you may have guessed, the world's most peopled continent is also home to the world's greatest number of Internet users. There are almost **four billion** people in Asia. Of these, over **a billion** are Internet users. That's almost as many users as the rest of the world put together!

27. **Europe**. The people of Europe account for around 22 per cent (more than one-fifth) of all Internet users worldwide. That's almost as many as North and South America *combined*.

28. **North America**. With their huge land area, huge cities and reputation for modern, luxury lifestyles, you might expect that Americans and Canadians would make up more than 6 per cent of all Internet users. But there are over ten times as many Asians as there are Americans in the world, and almost twice as many people in South America, compared with the North.

29. **Africa**. Africa is the second most populated continent on the planet, but due to poverty, civil war and poor technological development in rural areas, less than 14 per cent of its people have access to the Internet. Over **a billion** people live there, but only **140,000** or so are regular Internet users.

30. **North America**. Although only the fifth largest continent (out of seven) in terms of population, North America has a higher level of Internet coverage than any other continent. Almost **80 per cent** of North Americans have access to the Internet.

# D: PICTURE PUZZLE 2

**Odd one out**

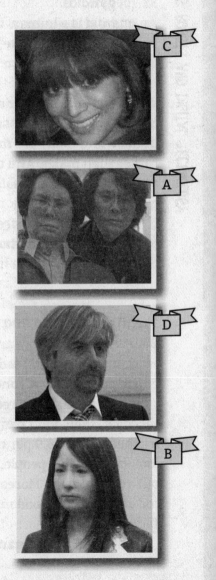

The odd one out is image **C**. This picture depicts a real person, but the 'people' in images A, B and D are all **geminoids** – remarkably realistic 'twin' androids built to look like their owners.

In fact, they were all built by robotics professor **Hiroshi Ishiguro** – pictured alongside his own **Geminoid HI-1**, in image A.

Image B shows **Geminoid-F**, and (believe it or not) image D is **Geminoid-DK** – perhaps the most advanced android built to date.

Image C is a photograph of Japanese pop star **Ayumi Hamasaki**. And she's human. Honest.

145

# E: MORE MEGA-BRAIN ANSWERS

### 31. (c) gynoids

An *android* is a human-like robot. In other words, one built to look and behave like a human being. The word comes from the Greek *andros* (meaning 'man') and *-oid* (meaning '-like').

But in truth, androids can be woman-like as well. In fact, some of the most advanced human-like robots in the world today are made to resemble females, rather than males. And technically speaking, a female android is called a *gynoid* – from the Greek word *gynos*, meaning 'woman'.

To qualify as an android (or gynoid), the robot has to *look* like a human (that means skin, hair and facial features) and *act* like a human too.

### 32. (d) about 9,000,000 (9 million)

Believe it or not, there are over **9 million** robots working in the world today. That's equivalent to the entire population of London.

If that seems like a recipe for a global robot takeover, then don't panic just yet. As we've already learned, about 99.9 per cent of these 9 million robots look nothing like people, so they'd have trouble hiding out and fitting in. Moreover, most of them aren't too clever. And a good number of them are bolted to factory floors.

More than three-quarters of all working robots are

**industrial robots**, working on assembly lines in car and electronics factories. Others help build precision instruments for scientists and surgeons, or mix and bottle medicines in pharmaceutical factories.

The second-largest group is **service robots**. These include robot drones and other aircraft used by the military, along with satellites, space probes and robot rovers used to explore other planets. There are also robot pickers on farms, surgical robots (controlled by human surgeons) in hospitals, robotic submersibles for deep-sea research and oil exploration, and even one or two robot cars and trains – autonomous vehicles that drive themselves.

### 33. (a) hard work

The word **'robot'** comes from the Czech word *robota*, meaning 'hard work', 'drudgery' or 'slave labour'. The first person to use it was Czech playwright **Karel Čapek**, in his 1921 play about machines built to help humans with boring, menial tasks (which later rose up and killed their masters, a common theme in science fiction ever since). He called these machines 'robots' (slaves), and the play was called *Rossum's Universal Robots*.

Twenty years later, science-fiction writer **Isaac Asimov** was the first person to use the term **'robotics'** to describe robot-building research and industry. He also created, for one of his stories in 1942, the *Three Laws of Robotics*, designed to ensure that all robots remained safe to be around, and to prevent a robotic uprising. These are:

1) A robot **may not harm a human being**, or by inaction allow a human being to be harmed.
2) A robot **must obey all orders** given to it by a human being (unless that order violates Law 1).
3) A robot **must try to protect itself** (unless that act violates Law 1 or Law 2).

Fortunately, we have yet to invent a robot intelligent enough to require these laws. But when we do perhaps Asimov's Three Laws will come in handy.

**34. (c) body, controller, sensors, actuators**
The basic parts needed to build a complete, working robot are:

1) **Body** (or **mechanism**). This describes the mechanical structures – gears, wheels, struts, panels, tubes and so on – that join together to create the robot's core. The body is equivalent to the **skeleton**, **ligaments**, **tendons** and **connective tissues** of a living animal or person.

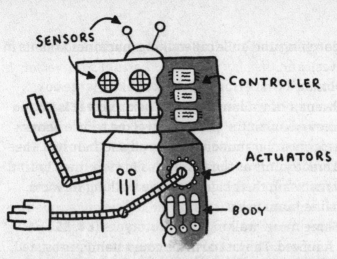

2) **Controller**. This is the robot's **brain**, which takes the form of an **integrated circuit**, one or more **microprocessor chips** or an entire **computer**.

3) **Sensors**. These are electronic devices that turn light, sounds and vibrations into electrical signals, allowing the robot to see, hear and feel its external environment. These are equivalent to **eyes**, **ears** and **touch receptors** in a human or animal body.

4) **Actuators**. These are the motors, pistons or other devices that actually move the parts of a robot's body around. They're equivalent to **muscles** in a human or animal body.

**35. (b) Honda**
**ASIMO**, probably the world's most famous humanoid robot, was built by engineers working for Japanese engineering company **Honda**. The company is better known for its cars and motorcycles, but began

149

researching and building walking, humanoid robots in 1986.

Honda's first effort, **EO**, looked like a large box with a pair of walking legs. The next three (**E1**, **E2** and **E3**) looked much the same, but walked a little better. Engineers programmed them to adjust their hip, knee and ankle joints as they walked, allowing them to find and maintain their balance while walking forward, much as humans do.

Three more 'walking box' prototypes (**E4**, **E5** and **E6**) followed. The last of these could stand unassisted, and walk up slopes and steps without falling over. Next came **P1**, **P2** and **P3** – which added an upper body and moving arms to the mix.

Redesigning **P3** led to the development of the first **ASIMO**, which was unveiled on 31 October 2000. At a friendly, child-sized, 130 cm tall, **ASIMO** (which stands for **Advanced Steps In Mobility**)

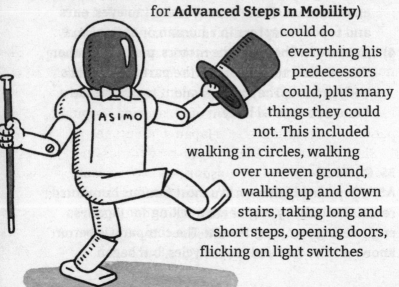

could do everything his predecessors could, plus many things they could not. This included walking in circles, walking over uneven ground, walking up and down stairs, taking long and short steps, opening doors, flicking on light switches and tapping on a computer keyboard.

The latest version of ASIMO can walk, jog, dance, speak, recognize faces, remember voices and obey a wide range of human vocal commands. How long, I wonder, before he can build a new version of himself?

## 36. (d) BIG DOG
**AIBO** was a robotic dog built by Sony, which first went on sale in 1999. Late-model AIBO pets could not only walk, sit and lie down just like a real dog, they could also follow coloured balls using head-mounted video cameras, and 'learn' (pre-programmed) tricks in response to commands from their owners. Over 150,000 AIBOs were sold, but sadly Sony stopped making them in 2007.

**PARO** is a cute, cuddly, robotic seal built by Japanese engineering company AIST. Modelled on a real seal pup, PARO can turn and wriggle his head and flippers, respond to touch, light and sounds using in-built sensors, turn toward sounds and recognize and respond to specific voices and commands. He's used mostly in the treatment of recovering hospital patients, in hospitals across Japan and Europe.

Similar in sprit is **PLEO** – a pet-robot dinosaur modelled on a baby *Camarasaurus*. **PLEO** can walk, learn pre-programmed commands and track coloured objects. He can also sense heat, light and pressure, recognize voices, turn towards sounds and figure out which way up he is, using positional sensors.

But unlike the other two robo-pets, each PLEO has a unique **personality**, which develops in response to both inbuilt traits and the care, attention or abuse he receives during his first few weeks of 'life'.

The Boston Dynamics **BIG DOG**, however, is *not* a robot pet. It's an experimental **military pack animal**, designed to carry heavy gear and ammunition over rough terrain in war zones. Shaped like a huge, headless Great Dane, the BIG DOG walks, trots and balances on four legs, and is difficult to knock over. Given a hefty shove or kick, it staggers sideways, but stays upright and if the BIG DOG is knocked down, it can actually get up again.

## 37. (d) all of the above

Believe it or not, robotics researchers have already built **robo-sharks**, **robo-lobsters** and, yes, even a **robot octopus**.

Full-sized, free-swimming **robotic sharks** have been built by engineers in Japan and Korea – partly

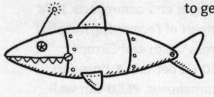

to get a better idea of how real sharks move so swiftly through the water. These sharks can sense the edges of a pool, turn, dive and surface, all by themselves. Thankfully, they do *not* eat people.

Scuttling **robot lobsters** were built as far back as 2003, designed to sniff out aquatic landmines. These robots mimic the movement of real lobsters – scuttling along on four pairs of legs, using their metal-detecting claw-pads and a pair of long, sensory antennae to detect dangerous undersea explosives.

More recently, a team of engineers at Harvard University built a **tentacled, aquatic robot** designed to mimic the squishy, slithering motions of an **octopus**. These **'softbots'** are made entirely from soft, transparent, silicone plastic and rubber, divided into individual muscle-like 'cells' filled with high-pressure liquids. By inflating and deflating these cells, an operator can make the softbot wriggle, crawl and twist much like an octopus or squid. Conventional 'hard' plastic or metal robots would have a very hard time with this.

## 38. (a) carrying stuff

Most of the world's 9,000,000 robots work in factories, and by far the most common task for industrial robots is **carrying stuff**.

Around **40 per cent** of all industrial robots are used to **shift**, **stack**, **sort**, **convey** and **handle goods**. What they carry depends on the industry. In pharmaceutical factories, it's pills and pill bottles. In the food industry, it's food, flavourings and packaging. In the automotive industry, it's vehicles and vehicle parts. Some of the largest robots in the world (including the five-tonne Kuka TITAN robot) can pick up entire cars and truck engines.

Another **30 per cent** of industrial robots are **welders**. Using gas or electricity, they heat and bind metal parts together non-stop, all day, in conditions that would prove dangerous for human workers.

Another **10 per cent** are **assemblers**. This type of robot is common in car factories – shifting heavy metal doors into place, threading rods and axels, and pressing parts together so that they can be welded, riveted or fixed in place by human workers or other robots.

The remainder are **processing robots** that take on a wide variety of tasks, including spray-painting, gluing, sealing, cutting, etching, high-pressure cleaning and more.

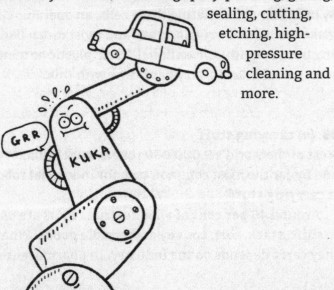

### 39. (b) bomb disposal

When it comes to military duty, robots certainly do their part. There are almost 10,000 robots serving in the US armed forces alone.

The vast majority of these are **Explosive Ordnance Disposal** (**EOD**) robots, used to locate and destroy bombs, landmines and other explosive devices. Operated by remote control, EOD 'bots' are the first in harm's way when a suspicious package or vehicle is spotted. Most rumble along on tank tracks, allowing them to move over uneven, rocky terrain. A video camera feeds information about the bomb back to the handler and disposal team standing by.

While they're rarely used to *defuse* bombs (this is a fiddly business), EOD bots can be used to **inspect** devices. Sometimes, a robot arm is used to open a door, prise open a package or shift a suspected bomb to a safer location. Occasionally, they're used to detonate bombs that are too difficult or dangerous to deal with any other way. (But since EOD bots themselves are pretty expensive, this is never the first option!) EOD bots like this save thousands of lives every year.

Another common class is the **aerial robot** – which includes Unmanned Aerial Vehicles (UAVs) and reconnaissance drones used to locate (and sometimes destroy) hostile targets. These include the fearsome **Predator**, **Reaper** and **Global Hawk** UAVs.

## 40. (d) he's the world's first cyborg

Kevin Warwick – Professor of Cybernetics at the University of Reading, England – is the world's first self-proclaimed cyborg. He's part man, part machine.

A **cyborg** is a **living organism** with **artificial** (electronic or robotic) **enhancements**. And Kevin Warwick is just that. In 1998, as part of his own research project entitled **Project Cyborg**, he implanted an electronic RFID (or Radio-Frequency Identification) chip into his own arm, to see if his body would accept it, and to see if the chip would still work after a month or so inside his body. It did. By waving his arm, he could use the signal transmitted from the chip to open computer-controlled doors and light switches.

Four years later, he went further – inserting an electrode array into his arm, which attached to a circuit-covered glove worn over his hand. This formed a direct interface between his nervous system and the electronics on the glove. Not only did his body accept the implant, he successfully used it to connect to the Internet and control a robot arm **over 3,000 miles away**, at a robotics lab in New York.

This, say the experts, is just the beginning of cybernetics. Soon, there will be cyborgs everywhere – watching TV through their optic nerves, accessing the Internet directly through their brains and controlling their cars and home appliances through the power of thought alone.

# TECHNO PUZZLER SOLUTION

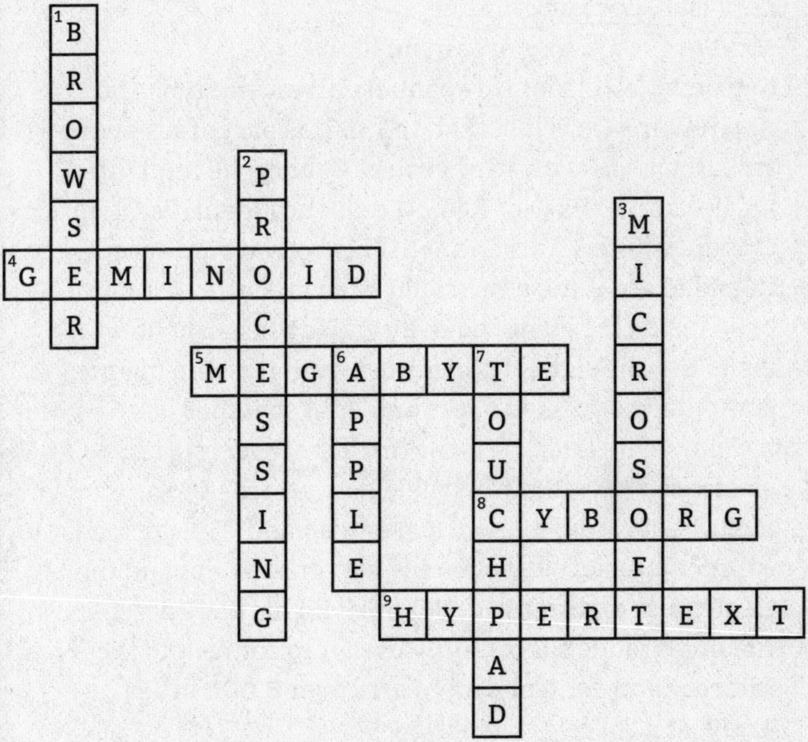
1 BROWSER
2 PROCESSING
3 MICROSOFT
4 GEMINOID
5 MEGABYTE
6 APPLE
7 TOUCHPAD
8 CYBORG
9 HYPERTEXT

# ANSWERS

## PART FOUR: ANIMALS AND ANIMAL BEHAVIOUR

# SUPERGEEK: ANSWERS

>>>>>>>>>>>>>>>>>>>>>>>>>>>>>>>>>>>

## A: MEGA-BRAIN ANSWERS

**1. (b) sea lettuce**

**Sea urchins**, **sea cucumbers** and **sea squirts** are all aquatic animals, while sea lettuce is a type of aquatic plant.

Zoologists divide the animal kingdom into larger and smaller groups, based on their shared characteristics. Just as different **species** can belong to the same **family**, each family also belongs to a larger **order**, each order of animals to an even larger **class**, and each class to a **phylum**. The phylums (or more correctly **phyla**) are the largest groupings within the animal kingdom, and animals of different phyla are *very*, *very* different from each other.

For example, spiders, insects, centipedes, millipedes, crabs, lobsters and shrimp are very different animals. They belong to differing families, orders and classes of animal. But they're all part of the phylum **Arthropoda**.

Sea urchins and sea cucumbers belong to another phylum entirely – **Echinodermata**. Echinoderms (which also include starfish and brittle stars) have a skeleton made of chalky (calcium carbonate) plates, arranged into five identical parts round a central point. **Urchins** use a covering of hard, sharp spines for

>>>>>>>>>>>>>>>>>>>>>>>>>>>>>>>>>>>>>>>>>>>>

defence against predators. **Sea cucumbers** lack spines, but most release a toxic slime to make them seem less tasty to fish and crabs.

Tube-shaped **sea squirts** (or **tunicates**) look a bit like sea cucumbers, but actually belong to yet another phylum – **Chordata**. All **chordates** develop a spine-like rod called a notochord at some stage in their life cycle. Sea squirts only have this when they are free-swimming larvae. Later, they settle on rocks or coral reefs and filter their food from the water, by sucking and squirting it through their bodies.

Believe it or not, *all* **vertebrate** animals – including **fish**, **frogs**, **newts**, **cats**, **dogs**, **horses**, **bats**, **bears** and **human beings** – are chordates too. All these animals have notochords that develop into hard, segmented **backbones** later on.

> So, you and all other humans are related to sea squirts. Bet you didn't know that when you woke up this morning . . .

## 2. (b) jellyfish

Jellyfish belong to the phylum **Cnidaria**, which also includes **sea anemones** and **corals**. Cnidarians are tube-or bell-shaped aquatic animals with a ring of stinging tentacles round their mouths. **Corals**, **anemones** and **polyps** attach themselves to rocks or reefs, stinging and eating anything foolish enough to brush against their tentacles.

**Jellyfish**, on the other hand, spend at least part of their lives swimming free in the ocean – squeezing water from their bell-shaped bodies to change depth, move around and swarm together. Like their bottom-dwelling cousins, though, jellyfish don't actually *swim after* things. Instead, they drift and swarm about, waiting for fish, plankton and small crustaceans to blunder into their stinging tentacles.

All jellyfish tentacles contain stinging cells called nematocytes. Depending on the class of jellyfish, this venom may be **harmless** to humans, or it may be **painful**, **paralysing** or even **deadly**.

## 3. (d) 90 per cent

**Insects** are by far the most common animal species on the planet. There are well over a **million** known species of insect, and those are just the ones that scientists have had time to discover and give names to. New insect species are discovered somewhere in the world almost every day, and the true number is thought to be more like **10 million**. With an estimated 11 million animal species living on the planet, that means over 90 per cent of all animal species are likely to be insects.

HEAD

THORAX

ABDOMEN

All insects are **Arthropods** (members of the phylum **Arthropoda**), belong to the family **Insecta** and share a few common features. For starters, their bodies are divided into three main **segments** – the **head**, **thorax** and **abdomen**. Typically, they are small, and they reproduce very quickly, allowing them to grow in number rapidly.

**4. (b) ladybird**

Although people tend to call all insects 'bugs', ladybirds, beetles, flies and most other types of insect are not really bugs at all. True **bugs** only belong to one order of insects – the **Hemiptera**. True bugs have two pairs of wings and (as we've just learned) tube-shaped mouthparts, which they use to suck up sap or blood.

Here are a few of the more common families of bug:

- **Pond skaters (Gerridae)**, which skate across the surface of freshwater rivers, lakes and ponds.
- **Aphids (Aphididae)** and **plant bugs (Miridae)**. Tiny, dot-like **aphids** (also called blackflies and greenflies) eat the leaves and stems of plants, and are the scourge of gardeners across the globe. **Plant bugs** are slightly larger, and feed on fruit, crop plants and other, smaller insects.
- **Assassin bugs (Reduviidae)**, which live in the tropics, feeding on other bugs and on the blood of animals. Some also carry nasty, blood-borne diseases.

- **Stink bugs (Pentatomidae).** Also known as shield bugs, these shield-shaped bugs release a foul-smelling chemical from their thorax when disturbed, repelling predators. In the south-east Asian country of Laos, however, they are considered a fragrant and delicious snack.
- **Cicadas (Cicadidae).** Arguably the world's noisiest insect, cicadas lay their eggs in plant roots, and the larvae may stay underground for up to 17 years before turning into large, airborne adults.

## 5. (a) worms

**Nematodes**, otherwise known as **roundworms**, are tiny, parasitic worms that live inside almost every plant and animal on the planet.

There are so many, in fact, that if you were to suddenly make everything else in the world invisible, you could still make out the outline of every tree, every plant and every large animal on the planet, just by seeing the millions of nematodes that occupy their bodies. *That's* how many there are.

Nematodes all belong to the phylum Nematoda, which includes hookworms, pinworms, threadworms and more. While all are **parasitic** (meaning that they must live inside the body of a host animal in order to feed themselves and reproduce), most species are not actually *harmful* to their hosts. Some species, however, cause **diseases** in plants or animals. These include **coffee rust** and **berry rust** in plants, and intestinal **roundworm**, **hookworm**, **ascariasis** and **trichosis** in humans. Most **worming** medicines for pet cats and dogs are also designed to kill off harmful nematodes.

## 6. (c) hippos

Modern whales are actually more closely related to hippos than they are to large marine fish-like sharks and rays. Whales are warm-blooded, air-breathing mammals and although they are not descended directly from hippos, the hippopotamus is probably the closest living thing to the four-legged land mammals from which all modern whales evolved.

There are two major types of whales – **baleen whales** and **toothed whales**.

**Baleen whales (Mysticeti)** get their name from the 100–400 horny **baleen plates** attached to their upper jaws, which they use to filter plankton from seawater. Baleen whale species include the **fin whale**, **grey whale**, **right whale**, **bowhead whale** and the enormous **blue whale** – the largest animal ever to have lived on planet Earth.

**Toothed whales (Odonticeti)** are carnivorous **hunters**, with rows of conical **teeth** more suited to hunting fish and larger prey. These include **beluga**, **sperm**, and **pilot whales**, along with the smaller, faster

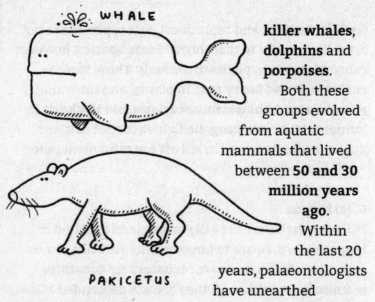

WHALE

PAKICETUS

killer whales, dolphins and porpoises.

Both these groups evolved from aquatic mammals that lived between **50 and 30 million years ago**.

Within the last 20 years, palaeontologists have unearthed complete fossilized skeletons of these ancestral 'pre-whales', which prove they existed and show us what they might have looked like.

The aquatic **dorudon** looked like a porpoise, but had stubby feet and toes sticking out of its streamlined body, about where the hips should be.

The **ambulocetus** ('walking whale') had four stubby legs and webbed feet, and probably spent at least some of its time out of the water, as modern sea otters do.

The **pakicetus** looked more like a skinny-legged hippo with a pointed snout. It walked on land on four, fully developed legs and hunted in and out of the water. The closest living relative of pakicetus is the hippo. So hippos, in turn, are the closest thing we have to prehistoric walking whales.

## 7. (c) Carnivora

Giant panda, sea otters, walruses and badgers are all members of the order **Carnivora**. You've probably heard the word 'carnivore' (meaning meat-eater) before. Some primates (monkeys and apes) are carnivorous, as are many birds and reptiles. But zoologically speaking, Carnivora are **mammals** of the order Carnivora, most of which have **forward-facing eyes**, powerful **jaws**, tough **claws** and sharp **teeth** – all adaptations for killing and shredding meaty prey.

The major families of Carnivora are **cats**, **dogs**, **hyenas**, **bears**, **raccoons**, **civets** and **mustelids**.

The **cat** family (**Felidae**) includes huge, fearsome cats like **lions**, **tigers**, **leopards**, **jaguars** and **cheetahs**, and smaller species like **servals**, **bobcats**, **ocelots**, **wildcats** and (of course) **domestic cats**.

The **dog** family (**Canidae**) includes not only all **dogs** and **wolves**, but also **foxes**, **jackals**, **dingoes**, **dholes** and **coyotes**. **Hyenas** and **aardwolves** are in a family all their own (**Hyenidae**), quite separate from the canids.

The **bear** family (**Ursidae**) includes **black bears**, **brown bears** (including grizzlies and Kodiaks), **sun bears**, **sloth bears**, **polar bears** and **giant pandas**. Bears are more closely related to dogs than any other carnivore family.

The **raccoon** family (**Procyontidae**) includes not just **raccoons**, but also rarer carnivores like the **coati**, **kinkajou** and **red panda**.

The **civet** family (**Viverridae**) includes the **agile**, cat-like **civets, genets** and **mongoose** and the sociable (but wary) **meerkat**.

The last major family of carnivores, the **mustelids (Mustelidae)** includes large land-based hunters like **badgers** and **wolverines**, along with the smaller **stoats, weasels, ferrets, martens, minks** and **skunks**, and the semi-aquatic **otters** and **sea otters**.

## 8. (d) their tails are different shapes

Manatees and dugongs are marine mammals of the order **Sirenia**. They are named after the **sirens** of Greek mythology – beautiful women who sang sweet songs that drew in sailors, drove them mad, and made them wreck their ships on rocks. In truth, they look more like seals or cows than beautiful ladies, which has earned them their more common name – **sea cows**.

Like cows, manatees and dugongs are **herbivores**, and spend much of their time grazing. But rather

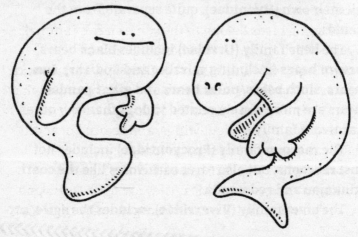

than grass, they eat seaweed, kelp and other aquatic plants – holding the leaves with their front flippers, and nibbling bits off with their flexible lips. They both have tiny eyes, no external ears, dense bones, bulbous bodies and thick skin. They both live in shallow waters or estuaries, and both are threatened by boat traffic and human hunters.

The main difference between manatees and dugongs is the shape of their tails. While manatees have flat, **rounded paddles**, dugongs have **crescent-shaped *fluked* tails** – more like those of a whale. They also live in different parts of the world – manatees in the coastal Atlantic, and dugongs in the coastal Pacific and Indian Ocean.

## 9. (b) owl

**Barn**, **burrowing**, **spectacled** and **snowy** are all **owl** species. (Although there *is* also a **spectacled bear** and a **spectacled bat**.

All living **birds** belong to the same class of animals – **Aves** – which includes families as diverse as **hummingbirds**, **kingfishers**, **pigeons**, **parrots**, **hawks**, **cranes** and **gulls**. Within this class, **owls** belong to the order **Strigiformes** – an order of deadly, nocturnal hunters that fly on silent wings, and see and hear *all* that scampers and hops in the forest.

**Barn owls** (*Tyto alba*) can be found on every continent except Antarctica. They are agile flyers and expert hunters, and are easily recognized by their long legs and pale, heart-shaped faces.

**Burrowing owls** (*Athene cunicularia*) use their long legs and sharp claws to dig holes in the ground, rather than build a tree nest, as other owls do. They're found throughout North and South America.

**Spectacled owls** (*Pulsatrix perspicillata*) have black-feathered heads, and faces with a ring of white round the eyes, making them look like sinister schoolteachers. They live in Central and South America, and hunt crabs and crayfish as well as rodents and rabbits.

**Snowy owls** (*Nyctea scandiaca*) live throughout the Arctic and subarctic regions of Russia, Europe and North America.

## 10. (d) they're all invertebrates

**Lobsters**, **earthworms** and **tarantulas** are all invertebrates – meaning that they lack a bony **spine** or **vertebral column**.

All **arthropods** are invertebrates, as they develop a tough, outer **exoskeleton** rather than the stiff **endoskeleton** of vertebrate animals. This goes for all insects, along with **arachnids** (spiders and scorpions), **crustaceans** (lobsters, crabs and shrimp), and **molluscs** (snails, squid, octopuses and shellfish).

**Earthworms** belong to the invertebrate phylum

**Annelida.** Neither they nor any other type of worm has a backbone, either. In fact, *most* animals are invertebrates. **Ninety-eight to ninety-nine per cent** of all known animal species lack a spine.

## B: PICTURE PUZZLE 1

**What is it?**

A – **Binturong**

B – **Narwhal**

C – **Pangolin**

D – **Sea Slug**
(Nudibranch)

# C: QUICK-FIRE ANSWERS

11. **Mammal**. The **aye-aye** (*Daubentonia madagascariensis*) is a rare species of nocturnal lemur that lives only on the island of Madagascar.
12. **Bird**. **Shrikes** are mid-sized perching birds of the family **Laniidae**. They've been nicknamed '**butcher birds**', thanks to their nasty habit of catching insects, impaling them on thorny bushes, and ripping bits off them, a little at a time.
13. **Mammal**. The **dik-dik** is a tiny antelope that lives in the savannahs and bushlands of Africa. At just 30–40 cm (14–16 inches) tall and weighing less than 7.5 kilograms (16 pounds), they're little bigger than a large house cat. They get their name from the high-pitched sounds (*dik-dik! dik-dik!*) that females make when threatened or alarmed.
14. **Fish**. **Groupers** are weighty, wide-mouthed sea fish. The largest species can reach over **a metre (three feet)** in length, and weigh over **100 kilograms (220 pounds)** – as much as a bodybuilder or heavyweight boxer!
15. **Insect**. **Mantids** are slow-moving predatory insects of the family **Mantidae**, the most famous of which is the sinister **praying mantis**. They range in size from less than **eight centimetres (three inches)** to more than **30 centimetres (12 inches)** long, and come in a wide range of bright colours. Some are also cannibals! Female praying mantises famously turn and bite the heads off their mates,

immediately after coupling. They don't do this just to be nasty. They actually *eat* the head, providing a nutritious meal to fuel all the egg-laying to come. I'm sure the males feel a *lot* better knowing this.

16. **8**. Scorpions, spiders, and other **arachnids** have **four** pairs of legs, so **eight** in total. In scorpions, the front two turn into pincers. In spiders, they do not.

17. **10**. Almost all crabs and lobsters have **five pairs** of jointed legs, so **ten** in total. The foremost pair develop into grasping pincers or claws, while the others are used for walking.

18. **14**. Almost all species of **woodlouse** have **seven pairs** of legs, so **fourteen** in total. Woodlice are actually **crustaceans**, more closely related to ocean-dwelling crabs and lobsters than to land insects like ants and beetles. Interestingly, only a **few** woodlouse species can roll themselves into a ball. Most cannot.

19. **6**. **Fleas** are tiny, wingless insects of the genus (or small family) **Siphonaptera**. Like all insects, they have three pairs of segmented legs, so six in total. All fleas have straw-like, tubular mouthparts which they jab into an animal's skin in order to suck its blood.

20. **6**. Beetles are by far the largest group of insect species. Over **40 per cent** of all insects – almost **half a million** species – are beetles. Like all insects, beetles have three pairs of legs, so six in total, beneath their tough, upper **carapace**. Most, but not all, beetles can fly.

21. **Australia**. Spiny echidnas are small anteaters of the **Tachyglossidae** family. Echidnas are **monotremes** – egg-laying mammals related to the weird and wonderful **platypus**. They lay leathery, soft-shelled eggs, but also suckle their young with milk after they are hatched. Aside from echidnas and platypuses (yes, platypuses, *not* platypi), no other animal lays eggs *and* produces milk. It's either one or the other.

22. **Arctic**. The **wolverine** (*Gulo gulo*) is the largest and most fierce member of the weasel family. In fact, it's one of the most fierce animals on the planet – regularly standing its ground against far larger animals. Wolverines have even been known to **fight grizzly and polar bears** over a fresh kill (with varying degrees of success).

23. **Africa**. The **mandrill** (*Mandrillus sphinx*) is the world's largest monkey, and also one of the most colourful. Male mandrills have **bright blue, hairless muzzles**, a **bright red stripe** running the length of the **nose**, and a **bright yellow mane** and beard. This is matched at the (ahem) *opposite* end by a hairless **bright-blue-and-red bottom**, framed with a yellow 'bottom mane'.

24. **Asia**. The **green water dragon** (*Physignathus cocincinus*), also known as the **Chinese water dragon**, **Thai water dragon** or **Asian water dragon**, is found throughout southeast Asia. They are large, bright-green, lizard-like reptiles which grow up to a metre (three feet) long, including their

tails. Most live in the forests of China, Thailand, Vietnam and Laos, hunting insects in the treetops and small fish in forest rivers. When threatened by a predator, they drop from their tree branches into the rivers below, where they can stay underwater for up to half an hour.

25. **Africa**. The **boomslang** (*Dispholidus typus*) is a large, venomous snake, native to Africa, south of the Sahara desert. Its name means 'tree snake' in Afrikaans and, true to its name, it lurks in treetops waiting for prey animals to come by. Boomslangs kill with a single, venomous bite. Their venom contains a powerful **haemotoxin** which stops the victim's blood from clotting, resulting in death from internal (or external) bleeding.

26. **Ape**. **Siamangs** are tailless gibbons native to Sumatra and Malaysia. They're noisy, hairy apes with a balloon-like throat pouch that inflates to help them howl and hoot.

27. **Rodent**. The **coypu** (*Myocastor coypus*) is a large, beaver-like **river rat** native to South America, but also found in smaller numbers in parts of Europe, Africa and North America. They grow up to 60 cm (24 inches) long, and are considered pests, since they destroy hundreds of acres of marshland every year in their non-stop munching of aquatic plants.

28. **Rodent**. The **capybara** (*Hydrochoerus hydrochaeris*) is the world's largest living rodent, and like the coypu, it is native to South America. Large males grow up to **140 cm (four feet)** long,

and weigh over **70 kilograms (150 pounds)**. That's one *serious* rat.

29. **Reptile**. The **tuatara** is a reptile of the family **Sphenodontidae** – the last surviving member of an order of dinosaur-like reptiles. Although not technically correct, some zoologists have called it 'the last living dinosaur'. It's an entirely different animal to lizards and other living reptiles.

30. **Cat**. The **jaguarundi** (*Herpailurus yaguarondi*) is a smallish **jungle cat** native to Central and South America. Looking much like a mini (house-cat sized) panther, it has grey or reddish-brown fur, and hunts **birds**, **reptiles** and **small monkeys** in its rainforest home. They also dive into rivers to catch **fish** – earning them the nickname '**otter cats**'.

## D: PICTURE PUZZLE 2

**Odd one out**

The odd one out here is: B – **horseshoe crab**. The others are all *crustaceans* whereas the horseshoe crab is not. In fact, the horseshoe crab is an entirely different type of animal, in a separate class of its own: **Merostomata** – one that is more closely related to land-dwelling *spiders* than to aquatic crabs and lobsters.

# E: MORE MEGA-BRAIN ANSWERS

**31. (a) shoots water at it**

**Archerfish** (also known as **spinner fish**) are the
William Tells of the fishy world. They live in freshwater
rivers and swamps throughout southeast Asia and
northern Australia, hunting spiders and insects that
perch in branches above the water.

There are at least seven species of archerfish, all of
which belong to the family **Toxotidae**. All of them have
impressive aim, and a unique way of bringing down
prey. When an archerfish eyes a target, it takes aim,
fills its mouth with water, presses its tongue to the roof
of its mouth and squeezes its gills shut to fire a high-
pressure jet of water up to **two metres (six feet)** above
the water.

**32. (a) sponge**

**Sponges** are among the simplest, oldest and strangest
animals on the planet. Most non-biologists think of
them as undersea plants, but in fact, sponges are
aquatic animals belonging to the phylum **Porifera**.

All sponges are **simple, multicellular animals** that
lack **hearts**, **brains** and **stomachs**. In fact, they have **no**
circulatory system, **no** digestive system and **no** nervous
system at all.

In many ways, sponges are little more than **clusters
of animal cells** clumped together into a single body
to make feeding and reproducing a little easier. Being

barely multicellular makes sponges unique among the animals, and allows them to perform an impressive party trick no other animal could hope to do. Drop them in a whirling blender, and sieve the chopped-up pieces into a water-filled bowl, and after a while the chunks creep back together and form themselves back into a whole animal.

Incredible!

## 33. (d) all of the above

Carnivorous mammals tend to rely on stalking and pouncing, rather than venomous bites. For many years, it was thought that the **duck-billed platypus** was the only venomous mammal alive.

Male **platypuses** produce a mixture of toxic chemicals using special **crural glands** in each hind leg. They also have claw-like **spurs** on each hind foot, which delivers the venom via prods and scratches. The venom is painful, but not harmful to humans and other animals. And since only the males produce it, it seems unlikely that they use it for hunting or defence. Instead, the males use these toxic spurs on each other during the platypus mating season – stabbing and prodding other suitors in fights over females.

More recently, biologists have discovered that some species of **mole** and **shrew** produce venom too. While not deadly, their bites can paralyse worms and insects, making it easier for them to snag prey.

Depending on how you look at it, vampire bats could be considered venomous mammals too. Their bites contain anticoagulant chemicals that stop blood from clotting. Their victims rarely (if ever) bleed to death, since the bats only lap up a few millilitres of blood each night. But still - that's one more venomous mammal on the list.

### 34. (d) go snorkelling

**Tapirs** are hairy, pig-like, hoofed mammals belonging to the order **Perissodactyla**. Most live in the forests of central and South America, although one species (the **Malayan tapir**) still lurks in the forests of Malaysia.

Tapirs have large, heavy, pig-like bodies mounted on skinny legs. *Unlike* pigs, however, they have stubby, movable **trunks** on the end of their snouts – like those of an elephant, only shorter. Like elephants, tapirs use their bendy nose-parts to clutch at vegetation, and shovel food into their mouths. But the tapir's trunk has another, more interesting use . . .

Tapirs are good swimmers, and are never found far

from water. This is because the water is their only real line of defence against jaguars and humans. When threatened, a tapir will take to the water and swim to safety. If the predator is too close, a tapir may *hide* underwater, using its stubby trunk as a **snorkel**. They learn to do this from a very young age, and mothers and calves will often hide and snorkel side by side.

## 35. (b) by suffocation

Contrary to popular belief, giant snakes like **pythons** and **boa constrictors** do not actually *crush* their victims to death. Rather, they coil themselves round their prey and tighten their grip, little by little, until the victim is unable to breathe in, and **suffocates**.

There are around 30 python species, most of which live in **Africa**, **Asia** and **Australia**. Large pythons mostly eat small mammals and birds, but have been known to bring down **deer**, **crocodiles** and (occasionally) **people**.

**Boas** live mostly in **Central** and **South America**, occupying the places in which pythons are absent. Like pythons, they kill by **constricting** their coils and **suffocating** their prey. Interestingly, while pythons lay **eggs**, boas give birth to **live young**.

Another famously large snake species, the **anaconda**, is also native to South America. Anacondas can reach lengths of **10 metres (33 feet)** or more, and tend to be heavier than most boas and pythons. They not only kill by suffocation but **drown** their prey too.

## 36. (b) tiger

While **lions**, **hyenas** and **chimpanzees** all hunt in packs, tigers are mostly solitary animals that may *travel* together as a small family, but always *hunt* alone.

**Tigers** are the largest members of the cat family, outweighing **lions** by **50 kilograms (100 pounds)** and measuring **30 cm (a foot)** longer from nose to tail. For the most part, lions prowl the wide, flat **savannahs** of Africa, while tigers prowl the dense **forests** of Asia.

These different environments have led tigers and lions to adopt very different lifestyles. Catching speedy **gazelles**, **wildebeest** and other **herding animals** on open plains and grasslands is tricky. It's hard to hide from an entire herd of wary animals. To counter this, lions hunt in packs (or **prides**), which **stalk together**, **attack together** and **surround** one or two slower, weaker animals – **separating** them from the safety of the herd, and bringing them down.

**Hyenas** spend as much time scavenging from lions as they do hunting for themselves. But when they do

hunt they do it in **packs**, just like lions. While they can't sprint and pounce like lions, they are incredible **long-distance runners**. So once the trap is sprung and one animal is separated from the herd, hyena packs will lope after it for miles and miles, until it eventually becomes exhausted and collapses.

**Chimpanzees** don't hunt often – spending much of their time eating fruit and leaves. But occasionally they too will hunt small colobus monkeys – chasing them through the trees and ripping them apart with their bare hands! Chimps work together in packs (or **troops**) to surround their prey and close in on one or two slower, weaker victims.

**Tigers**, however, do not bother with pack hunting. Instead, they track and stalk wild deer and pigs through dense forest, where the thick tree cover helps them sneak within pouncing distance without being seen. As often as not, they kill with a single leap.

### 37. (c) pouches

All mammals have **hair**, **nipples** and (at least as embryos) **tails**. But only marsupial mammals have pouches in which they rear their young. This is part of what puts marsupials in their own, unique **order** of mammals.

So why don't other mammals have pouches like this? Well, pretty much all other mammals nourish their young in the womb with a **placenta**. The placenta is a fleshy organ filled with blood vessels that develops alongside an as-yet-unborn (or **embryonic**) mammal. Its job is to form a gateway between the mother's blood supply and that of the embryo, so that food, wastes and useful proteins can be passed back and forth.

The placenta helps feed the baby mammal until it has grown to a good size, and is ready to be born.

Marsupials, though, do not develop a placenta. With no placenta, the baby marsupial can't stay in the womb as long, and cannot fully develop before it is born. In a way, then, all marsupial mammals are born **prematurely**.

When a human baby (or farm animal) is born prematurely, we put it in an **incubator** to help keep it warm, and feed it milk from a bottle until it has developed to a good enough size. Pouches, then, are nature's incubators. Inside a kangaroo or opossum's pouch, a young, helpless marsupial can be kept warm and safe – with access to milk from the nipples inside – until it is big enough to hop and scurry about on its own.

IN: FOOD, OXYGEN, VITAMINS

OUT: WASTE

PLACENTA

FOETUS

**38. (d) Bengal, Siberian, Malayan and Indochinese**
All living **tigers** (*Panthera tigris*) are of the same
species. But there are nine officially recognized types
(or **subspecies**) of tiger, each with slightly different
adult sizes, coat markings, behaviours or geographical
homes.

The four most common subspecies are the **Bengal
tiger**, the **Siberian tiger**, the **Malayan tiger** and the
**Indochinese tiger**.

The remaining five subspecies of tiger are either
**critically endangered** or already **extinct. Sumatran
tigers** are the smallest and darkest of the tiger
subspecies. They live only on the Indonesian island of
Sumatra, where poachers and farmers almost wiped
them out once too. Today, less than **400** survive in the
wild.

South China tigers, once found
throughout China and eastern Asia,
now number less than 50 – all of
them in Chinese zoos. They will
most likely never return to the
wild.

And the **Bali tiger**, the **Javan
tiger** and the **Caspian tiger** are already lost to the
world. All three subspecies were declared **extinct** in the
middle of the twentieth century.

**39. (b) peacock**
While **penguins**, **kiwis** and **kakapos** are all genuinely
flightless birds, **peacocks** are *perfectly* capable of flight.

They just choose not to do it much, since their large, ungainly feathers make them clumsy and vulnerable in the air, compared with other birds.

**Penguins**, of course, lost the ability to fly when their wings evolved into stubby **flippers** more suited to swimming than gliding.

**Kiwis** are small, hairy, nocturnal birds native to New Zealand. With no large predators on the island for tens of thousands of years, kiwis had no need of flight feathers or powerful wings, and lost them over the course of time. Sadly, when Polynesian settlers arrived they brought with them cats, dogs, pigs, stoats and other animals that slaughtered the helpless, flightless kiwis, right across New Zealand. Today, they survive in low numbers, deep within the nation's forests.

**Kakapos** are nocturnal parrots native to New Zealand, which became flightless (and were almost wiped out) for much the same reasons as the kiwi. Today, less than 100 kakapos are thought to survive in the wild.

**40. (b) fierce snake**
The deadliest land snake in the world is not a **rattler**, a **cobra** or the infamous **black mamba**. It's actually the **inland taipan**, also known as the **fierce snake**.

A single fierce snake contains enough venom to kill **100 humans**, and its venom is **10 times** more powerful than that of a common rattlesnake, and **100 times** more powerful than that of a common cobra.

**King cobras'** bite is powerful enough to kill a

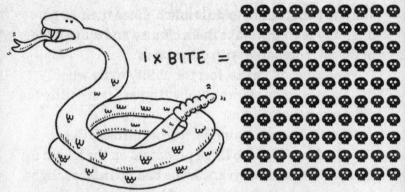

1 x BITE =

fully grown elephant. In humans, **50–60 per cent** of untreated bites lead to a coma, followed by death.

But the bite of the **black mamba** (*Dendroaspis polylepis*) is even worse. Left untreated, its bite kills **100 per cent** of its human victims.

**Rattlesnakes** belong to a separate family of serpents, the **Viperidae**, which also includes **adders**, **vipers** and **pit vipers**. Members of this family track their prey using heat-sensitive **pits** between their nostrils, and inject a powerful venom that prevents blood clotting – causing the victim to die of internal or external bleeding.

Snakes, eh? Not to be messed with.

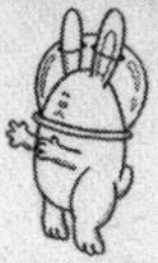

# ANIMAL PUZZLER SOLUTION

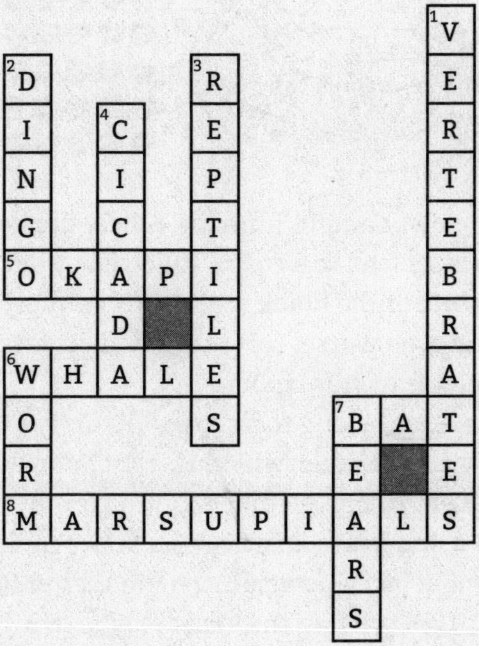
1 VERTEBRATES
2 DINGO
3 REPTILES
4 CICADA
5 OKAPI
6 WHALE
6 WORM
7 BAT
7 BEARS
8 MARSUPIALS

# HOW TO PLAY
# SUPERGEEK!

# The Rules

However you play the game, you'll need some sort of **timer** to limit the amount of time a player or team has to respond to each question. And if you want to play this book more than once you'll also need some **blank paper** and **pens**, so you can jot down the answers without scribbling all over the book. For team play, you might also need to nominate someone (the **SuperGeek! Quizmaster**) to ask the questions, to time the answers, to note the responses and to sum up the scores.

## CHAPTERS

The book is laid out in **four** chapters – each with a separate theme. Each **question chapter** has a corresponding **answer chapter** in the back half of the book.

Each question chapter features the same layout which goes like this:

- 10 multiple-choice mega-brain questions
- picture quiz 1
- 20 quick-fire questions
- picture quiz 2
- another 10 multiple-choice mega-brain questions
- crossword
- Top 10

The **crossword** and **Top 10**s are there just for fun.
There are no scores associated with these for normal
gameplay. The rest all feature in the game.

Make sure you leave *plenty* of time to read the
long answers, as there are loads of fascinating facts
in there and you'll learn tons just from going through
them.

(If you *don't* have time, and just want to play a
quick-fire game, you can always go back and read the
mega-brain answers later.)

If you're playing solo, you can expect to get through
each chapter (responding to questions, then reading
all the answers) in an hour or so. If you're playing in
teams, it might take a little longer – especially if your
team mates spend a long time arguing over the best
answer!

# SCORING

Scoring the game works more or less the same however
you decide to play.

That is:

**1 point** for every correct answer in the quick-fire and
mega-brain sections
• maximum score: **40 points**

**2 points** for every correct answer in Picture Puzzle 1
• maximum score: **8 points**

**1 point** for correctly identifying the odd one out in Picture Puzzle 2, and **1 extra point** if you can explain *why* it's the odd one out
• maximum score: **2 points**

Added together, this gives a maximum score of **50 points** per chapter. And since there are 4 chapters in total, the maximum score for the entire book is (50 X 4 =) **200 points**.

Once you have a total score for a chapter, you can see how you did, using the **SuperGeek! Scoring Scale** on page 198.

If you complete the entire book and score more than **180** points, you will have earned the title **SuperGeek**. Log on to www.glennmurphybooks.co.uk/supergeek and submit your name, home town and final SuperGeek! score, and you could earn a place on the **SuperGeek! Leaderboard** – updated regularly to show the Top 50 SuperGeeks worldwide. Just think – you could be the **next reigning WORLD CHAMPION of Geek**. Surely, there is no higher honour. Not even a Nobel Prize. After all, you only have to be good at **one** science subject to land one of those . . .

# GAME VERSIONS

Depending on how many players you have, there are four basic versions of the SuperGeek! game. Or rather, four ways to compete using the *SuperGeek!* book.

## Solo Play

- For this, you'll need a **stopwatch** or **countdown timer** set for 30 seconds, and (unless you just want to circle the answers on the page) a pen or pencil and paper for jotting down the answers.
- On one side of the page, write the numbers 1–20 and 'PP1' (for Picture Puzzle 1) in columns running down the page. On the back, write the numbers 21–40 and 'PP2'.
- Answer each question – reading the question, then starting the timer right away, so that you only have 30 seconds to choose your answer.
- Stop at the end of the chapter, and review the answers.
- Award yourself a mark out of 50, and consult the **SuperGeek! Scoring Scale** to see how you ranked.
- At this point, you can either move on to the next chapter, or leave it for another time – keeping your chapter score safe for future reference.
- Once you have completed all four chapters, add up your chapter scores and calculate your final SuperGeek! score. If you scored 180 or more, log on to www.glennmurphybooks.co.uk/supergeek and proclaim your brilliance to the world!

# Head-to-Head

- For this version of the game, you'll need someone to play against, head-to-head. You'll each need a paper and pen, labelled on each side with the question numbers for the chapter ahead.
- Go through each question, taking turns to read out the question options, and then setting off the 30-second timer.
- Each player writes down their own answer (keep it secret!), and play proceeds until you have completed all 40 questions (plus the two picture quizzes) and reached the end of the chapter.
- This done, the players swap answers sheets, and one player consults the answers, reading out the correct answers. Each player marks the other's answer (with a 1 for the right answer, 0 for the wrong answer, and a 2 for a correct answer on the picture quiz).
- Add up the scores to get the final chapter score, and see who won the round! You can also consult the **SuperGeek! Scoring Scale** to see how you both ranked.
- You can play the next chapter immediately, or save your score and play the next chapter another day. Add your chapter scores to get your final SuperGeek! score (out of 200), and submit your score to the SuperGeek! Leaderboard (www.glennmurphybooks.co.uk/supergeek) if either (or both!) of you scored 180 or more.

# Group/Team Play

- This version of the game is played when you have more than two players. For example, when you're playing as a family of four or five on a car trip, or you have three or more friends over for a SuperGeek! party. (Hey – if you're going to play, why not make a party out of it?)
- Players can play **individually** (with each person giving their **own** answers) or in **teams of two or three** players (with each **team** agreeing on **one** answer per question).
- Each individual player or team will need their own answer sheet (piece of paper labelled with the question numbers for each chapter), a pen to jot their answers down and something to lean on, like a clipboard or hardback book.
- The game works best if you can nominate one person to be Quizmaster. The Quizmaster does not play the game. If *everyone* wants to play, you can take turns being Quizmaster.
- In each round, the Quizmaster reads out the question (and answer options) and sets the timer running. If you're playing in teams, allow up to 60 seconds per question, to give time for the players within each team to decide whose answer is right!
- When the time is up, the Quizmaster moves on to the next question.
- Play continues until the players reach the end of the chapter. The players/teams swap answer sheets,

the Quizmaster reads out the correct answers from the answer chapter section, and each player/team marks each question with a 1 or 0. (Or for the Picture Puzzles only, 2.)

- This done, the players shout out their scores for that section, and the Quizmaster writes them down on his/her own piece of paper.

- Winners celebrate, losers mumble and you all decide if you want to play another chapter or leave the next one for another day.

- As before, if you can keep track of your chapter scores, you can add them to get a final SuperGeek! score, and players/teams can submit scores of 180+ to the **SuperGeek! Leaderboard** (www.glennmurphybooks.co.uk/supergeek).

# Classroom Challenge

- This version of the game is designed for entire classes (or 30–40 players) to play at once.

- At the beginning of the game, the players are split into two or more teams, and each team of 10–20 people chooses a **suitably awesome name** for itself. This is very important. After all, if your team is victorious, and ends up on top of the world SuperGeek! Leaderboard, you don't want a rubbish, wimpy name up there, do you?

- Each team needs a piece of paper to list their answers.

- From this point onward, the game proceeds just like

the team game described above, with the **teacher** (or other non-player nominated by the class) playing the role of Quizmaster throughout. The Quizmaster asks the questions and times the responses, giving each team up to 60 seconds to argue and jot down their answer.

- At the end of the chapter, the teams swap answer sheets, and the Quizmaster reads out the correct answers (allow plenty of time for this part). Once the teams are done marking each other's answers (1, 0 or 2), they give the answer sheets to the Quizmaster.
- The Quizmaster adds the scores for each team and declares the winners.
- Once more, if you can keep your chapter scores for each round, you can add them after all four rounds are complete to get your team's final SuperGeek! score.
- If your team scored 180 or more, log on to www.glennmurphybooks.co.uk/supergeek and submit your (awesome) team name and final score. If you rank in the Top 50 teams in the world, you will be placed on the SuperGeek! Leaderboard and revered by every geek on the Internet. Well, at least until someone beats you and knocks you off the list.

# SuperGeek! Scoring Scale

| Final Score | Chapter Score | Rank |
|---|---|---|
| 180–200 | 45–50 | **SuperGeek** |

**SuperGeek**

You have reached the very top of the geek food chain. Mere mortals cower at your magnificence, and geeks around the globe strive to be you, even if only for a minute. Congratulations, for YOU. ARE. A. SUPER. GEEK.

| 160–179 | 40–44 | **Elite Geek** |
|---|---|---|

**Elite Geek**

Lesser geeks grovel at your feet, hoping that scraps of knowledge will drop from your incredible brain. You are second only to the SuperGeek in your command of the Geekiverse.

| 140–159 | 35–39 | **Advanced Geek** |
|---|---|---|

**Advanced Geek**

You sit far above the average geek, with a mind for facts and an appetite for learning about the world. You are well on your way to geek greatness.

| | | |
|---|---|---|
| 100–139 | 25–34 | **Standard Geek** |

**Standard Geek**
You have an admirable grasp of all things science-y. Good job. But you'll have to learn a lot more if you're to join the geek elite.

| | | |
|---|---|---|
| 70–99 | 15–24 | **Wannabe Geek** |

**Wannabe Geek**
You want to be a geek, but you lack the required knowledge. Read some more Glenn Murphy books, then come back and try again.

| | | |
|---|---|---|
| 0–69 | 0–14 | **Noob** |

**Noob**
Hmmmm. You have a long way to go before you get to claim the title of 'geek'. Good effort, but must try harder.

For more information about Glenn Murphy books, including updates on new releases and titles, check out www.glennmurphybooks.co.uk, or 'Like' us on Facebook at www.facebook.com/GlennMurphyBooks.